NYSTCE®

Mathematics Practice Questions

Mometrix
TEST PREPARATION

Dear Future Exam Success Story

First of all, **THANK YOU** for purchasing Mometrix study materials!

Second, congratulations! You are one of the few determined test-takers who are committed to doing whatever it takes to excel on your exam. **You have come to the right place.** We developed these practice tests with one goal in mind: to deliver you the best possible approximation of the questions you will see on test day.

Standardized testing is one of the biggest obstacles on your road to success, which only increases the importance of doing well in the high-pressure, high-stakes environment of test day. Your results on this test could have a significant impact on your future, and these practice tests will give you the repetitions you need to build your familiarity and confidence with the test content and format to help you achieve your full potential on test day.

Your success is our success

We would love to hear from you! If you would like to share the story of your exam success or if you have any questions or comments in regard to our products, please contact us at **800-673-8175** or **support@mometrix.com**.

Thanks again for your business and we wish you continued success!

Sincerely,
The Mometrix Test Preparation Team

Printed in the United States of America

Table of Contents

Practice Test #1

1. A woman wants to park her 15-foot-long car in a garage that is 19 feet long. How far from the front of the garage will the front of her car need to be so that the car is centered on the floor of the garage?

a. 2 feet
b. $2\frac{1}{2}$ feet
c. 3 feet
d. $3\frac{1}{2}$ feet

2. A man looks out of a window of a tall building at a 45° angle of depression and sees his car in the parking lot. When he turns his gaze downward to a 60° angle of depression, he sees his wife's car. If his car is parked 60 feet from his wife's car, about how far from the building did his wife park her car?

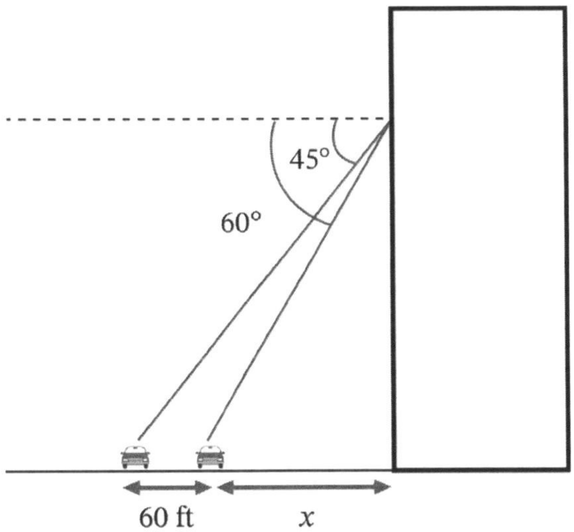

a. 163 feet
b. 122 feet
c. 82 feet
d. 60 feet

3. The velocity of a car which starts at position 0 at time 0 is given by the equation $v(t) = -t^2 + 8t$ for $0 \leq t \leq 8$. Find the position of the car when its acceleration is 0.

a. 64
b. $\frac{128}{3}$
c. 16
d. $\frac{56}{3}$

4. A developer decides to build a fence around a neighborhood park, which is positioned on a rectangular lot. Rather than fencing along the lot line, he fences x feet from each of the lot's boundaries. By fencing a rectangular space 141 yd^2 smaller than the lot, the developer saves \$432 in fencing materials, which cost \$12 per linear foot. How much does he spend?

a. \$160
b. \$456
c. \$3,168
d. The answer cannot be determined from the given information.

5. In a town of 6,089 people, about 80% of the population is over the age of 10. Of those, approximately 10% attend the local 4-year high school. If the number of students in each grade is about the same, how many 11th graders likely reside in the town?

a. Fewer than 100
b. Between 100 and 150
c. Between 150 and 200
d. More than 200

6. Ride Service A charges a flat rate of \$10 for the first 10 miles, plus 25 cents per mile for anything over 10 miles. Ride Service B charges 40 cents per mile. Both services charge the same for a trip that is how long?

a. 40 miles
b. 45 miles
c. 50 miles
d. 55 miles

7. Find $(g \circ f)(x)$ when $f(x) = 2x + 4$ and $g(x) = x^2 - 3x + 2$.

a. $4x^2 + 10x + 6$
b. $2x^2 - 6x + 8$
c. $4x^2 + 13x + 18$
d. $2x^2 - 3x + 6$

8. Approximate the area A under the curve by using left and right Riemann sums with $\Delta x = 1$.

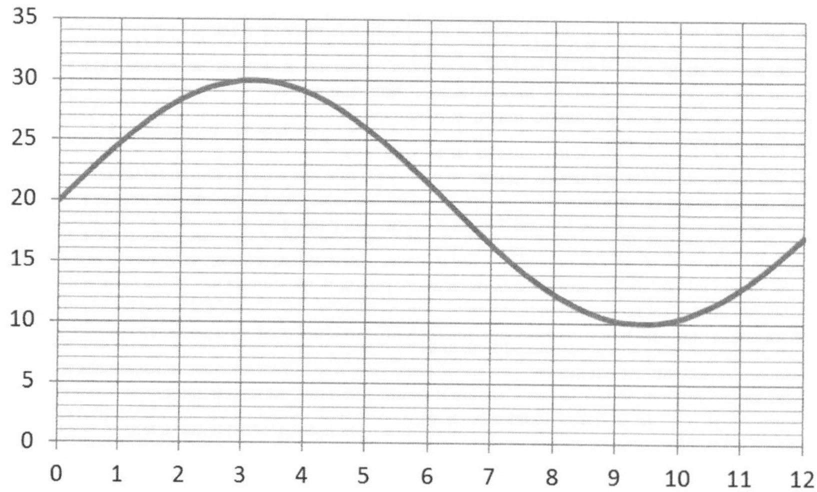

a. $209 < A < 211$
b. $230 < A < 235$
c. $238 < A < 241$
d. $246 < A < 250$

9. Solve $\csc^2 \theta = 2 \cot \theta$ for $0 < \theta \leq 2\pi$.

a. $\theta = \frac{\pi}{6}$ or $\frac{7\pi}{6}$
b. $\theta = \frac{\pi}{4}$ or $\frac{5\pi}{4}$
c. $\theta = \frac{3\pi}{4}$ or $\frac{7\pi}{4}$
d. $\theta = \frac{3\pi}{4}$ or $\frac{\pi}{6}$

10. Categorize the following statements as axioms of Euclidean, hyperbolic, or elliptical geometry.

I. If a point is not on a given line, exactly one line parallel to the given line can be drawn through the point.
II. If a point is not on a given line, an infinite number of lines parallel to the given line can be drawn through the point.
III. If a point is not on a given line, no lines parallel to the given line can be drawn through the point.

a.

Statement I	Elliptical geometry
Statement II	Euclidean geometry
Statement III	Hyperbolic geometry

b.

Statement I	Euclidean geometry
Statement II	Hyperbolic geometry
Statement III	Elliptical geometry

c.

Statement I	Hyperbolic geometry
Statement II	Elliptical geometry
Statement III	Euclidean geometry

d.

Statement I	Elliptical geometry
Statement II	Hyperbolic geometry
Statement III	Euclidean geometry

11. At today's visit to her doctor, Josephine was prescribed a liquid medication with instructions to take 25 cc's every four hours. She filled the prescription on her way to work, but when it came time to take the medicine, she realized that the pharmacist did not include a measuring cup. Josephine estimated that the plastic spoon in her desk drawer was about the same size as a teaspoon and decided to use it to measure the approximate dosage. She recalled that one cubic centimeter (cc) is equal to one milliliter (mL) but was not sure how many milliliters were in a teaspoon. So, she noted that a two-liter bottle of soda contains about the same amount as a half-gallon container of milk and applied her knowledge of the customary system of measurement to determine how many teaspoons of medicine to take. Which of these calculations might she have used to approximate her dosage?

a. $25 \times \frac{1}{1{,}000} \times \frac{2}{0.5} \times 16 \times 48$
b. $25 \times \frac{1}{100} \times \frac{0.5}{2} \times 16 \times 4 \times 12$
c. $\frac{1{,}000}{25} \times \frac{0.5}{2} \times 16 \times 4 \times 12$
d. $\frac{25}{1{,}000} \times \frac{1}{4} \times 16 \times 48$

12. A colony of bacteria are grown in a lab. After half an hour, the number of bacteria is determined to be 4×10^3. If the doubling time is 15 minutes, approximately how many bacteria should be counted after six hours of growth?

a. 2.6×10^8
b. 1.7×10^{10}
c. 3.2×10^{12}
d. 4.9×10^{14}

13. Solve the system of equations.

$$\begin{cases} 3x + 4y - z = 5 \\ -x + 2y + z = 0 \\ x + 2y + 2z = 2 \end{cases}$$

a. $(1, 0, -2)$
b. $\left(-\frac{1}{2}, 3, -4\right)$
c. $\left(1, \frac{1}{2}, 0\right)$
d. $\left(-\frac{1}{4}, 2, 1\right)$

14. Which of the following expressions is equal to $\sin\theta \sec\theta$?

a. $\cot\theta$
b. $\tan\theta$
c. $\csc\theta$
d. $\sec\theta - 1$

15. For which of these does a rotation of 45° about the center of the polygon map the polygon onto itself?

a. Square
b. Regular hexagon
c. Regular octagon
d. Regular decagon

16. Given: $f(x) = 10^x$. If $f(x) = 5$, which of these approximates x?

a. 100,000
b. 0.00001
c. 0.7
d. 1.6

17. If $\sin\theta = \frac{\sqrt{3}}{2}$ when $\frac{\pi}{2} < \theta < \pi$, what is the value of θ?

a. $\frac{\pi}{6}$
b. $\frac{3\pi}{4}$
c. $\frac{2\pi}{3}$
d. $\frac{5\pi}{6}$

18. Which of the following expressions gives the area A of the triangle below in terms of x? Note: The figure is not drawn to scale.

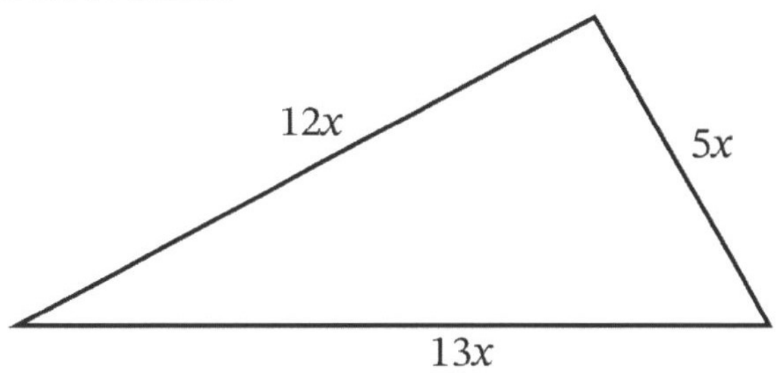

a. $30x^2$
b. $5\sqrt{3x^2 - 1}$
c. $\frac{x\sqrt{5x^2}}{12}$
d. $\frac{3x\sqrt{13x^2}}{25}$

19. If a square root of twice the sum of x and 6 is equal to half of x, which of these is a possible value of x?

a. 12
b. $\frac{3}{2}$
c. $-3i$
d. -3

20. If $f(x) = 3x^3 - x^2 + \frac{1}{2}$, what is $\lim_{h\to 0} \frac{f(1+h)-f(1)}{h}$?

a. $\frac{1}{2}$
b. 4
c. 7
d. 11

21. A rainbow pattern is designed from semicircles, as shown below.

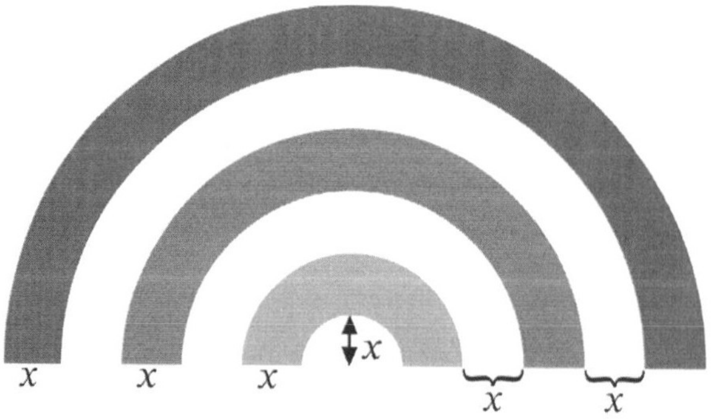

Which of the following gives the area A of the shaded region as a function of x?

a. $A = \frac{21\pi x^2}{2}$
b. $A = 21\pi x^2$
c. $A = 42\pi x^2$
d. $A = 82\pi x^2$

22. A circle is inscribed inside quadrilateral $ABCD$. $\overline{CD}$ is bisected by the point at which it is tangent to the circle. If $\overline{AB} = 14$, $\overline{BC} = 10$, $\overline{CD} = 8$, then which of the following statements is true?

a. $\overline{AD} = 11$
b. $\overline{AD} = 2\sqrt{34}$
c. $\overline{AD} = 12$
d. $\overline{AD} = 17.5$

Refer to the following for question 23:

Below are graphed functions $f(x) = a_1 \sin(b_1 x)$ and $g(x) = a_2 \cos(b_2 x)$; a_1 and a_2 are integers, and b_1 and b_2 are positive rational numbers.

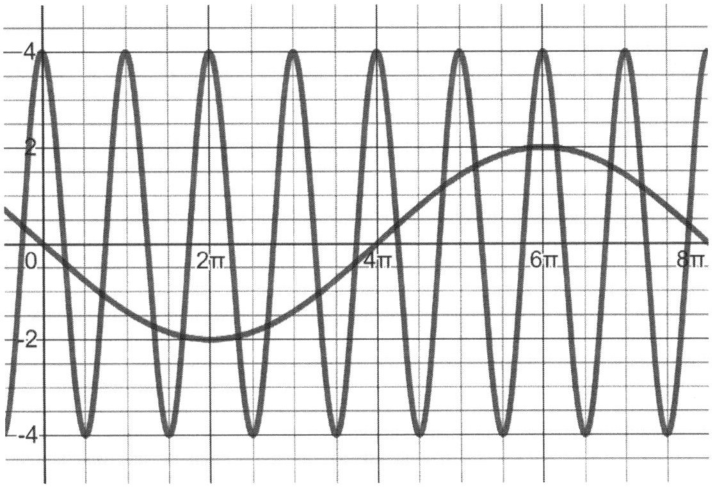

23. Which of the following statements is true?

a. The period of $f(x)$ is 8π.
b. The amplitude of the graph of $g(x)$ is 8.
c. $0 < b_2 < 1$
d. $b_2 = \pi$

24. Jamal plants a white petunia for every three red petunias in the flowerbed. If he plants 8 white petunias and r red petunias, which of the following equations is true?

a. $3r = 8$
b. $8r = 3$
c. $\frac{r}{3} = 8$
d. $r + 3 = 8$

25. Two companies offer monthly cell phone plans, both of which include free text messaging. Company A charges a $25 monthly fee plus five cents per minute of phone conversation, while Company B charges a $50 monthly fee and offers unlimited calling. At what total duration of monthly calls do both companies charge the same amount?

a. 500 hours
b. 8 hours and 33 minutes
c. 8 hours and 20 minutes
d. 5 hours

26. A manufacturer wishes to produce a cylindrical can which can hold up to 0.5 L of liquid. To the nearest tenth, what is the radius of the can which requires the least amount of material to make?

a. 2.8 cm
b. 4.3 cm
c. 5.0 cm
d. 9.2 cm

27. Sheila eats $\frac{1}{3}$ of a chocolate bar. Then, she eats an additional area $\frac{1}{3}$ the size of what she just ate. Next, she eats another area $\frac{1}{3}$ as large as the previous one. As she continues the process to infinity, what is the limit of the amount of the chocolate bar she eats?

a. $\frac{1}{3}$
b. $\frac{2}{3}$
c. $\frac{3}{4}$
d. $\frac{1}{2}$

28. If $f(x) = x + 3$ and $f(g(x)) = g(f(x))$, which of the following could be $g(x)$?

a. $-x$
b. $x - 4$
c. $3x$
d. e^x

29. Find the derivative of: $f(x) = e^{x^3 - x}$

a. $(3x^2 - 1)e^{3x^2 - 1}$
b. $e^{3x^2 - 1}$
c. $(3x^2 - 1)e^{x^3 - x}$
d. $3x^2 e^{x^3 - x}$

30. Which of these sets forms a group under multiplication?

a. $\{-i, 0, i\}$
b. $\{-1, 1, i, -i\}$
c. $\{i, 1\}$
d. $\{i, -i, 1\}$

31. What equation is graphed below?

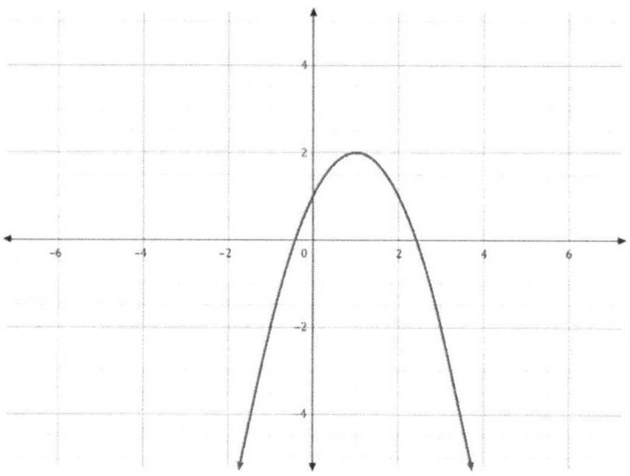

a. $y = -2x^2 - 2x + 1$
b. $y = -x^2 + 2x + 1$
c. $y = -x^2 - 2x + 2$
d. $y = -\frac{1}{2}x^2 - x + 2$

Refer to the following for question 32:

Consider the following graphic showing demographics of a high school with 1,219 total students:

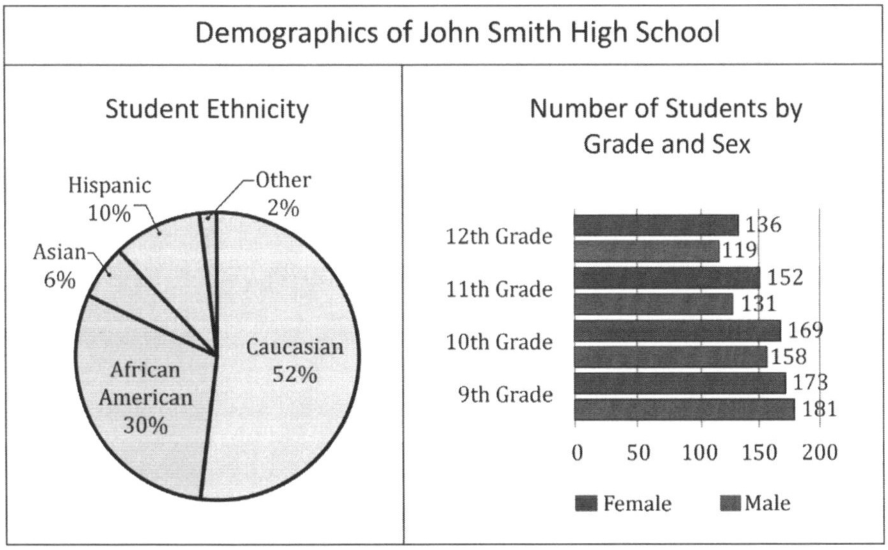

32. Compare the two quantities.

Quantity A	Quantity B
The percentage of Caucasian students	The percentage of female students, rounded to the nearest whole number

a. Quantity A is greater.
b. Quantity B is greater.
c. The two quantities are the same.
d. The relationship cannot be determined from the given information.

33. A dress is marked down by 20% and placed on a clearance rack, under a sign reading "Take an extra 25% off already reduced merchandise." What fraction of the original price is the final sale price of the dress?

a. $\frac{2}{5}$
b. $\frac{9}{20}$
c. $\frac{3}{5}$
d. $\frac{11}{20}$

34. If $3\log_3 y + \log_3 3 = 4$, what is $\log_y 243$?

a. 3
b. 5
c. 6
d. 9

35. If $f(x)$ and $g(x)$ are inverse functions, which of these is the value of x when $f(g(x)) = 4$?

a. -4
b. $\frac{1}{4}$
c. 2
d. 4

36. Which of these graphs is representative of the data set shown below?

3	2 5 5
4	1 3 6 6 7
5	2 7 8
6	0 5 6 6 8

KEY

$2|123 = 21, 22, 23$

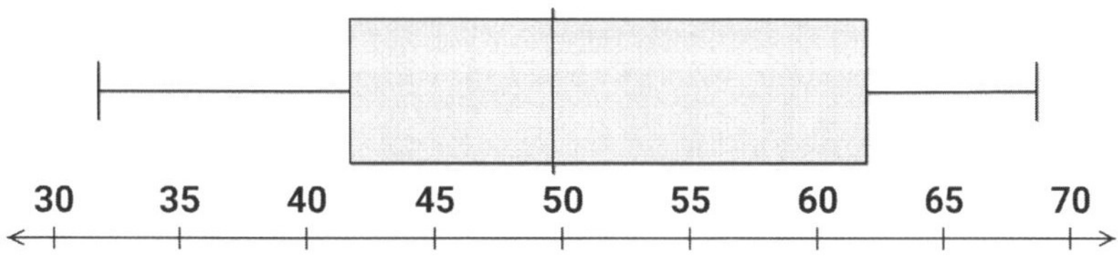

a.

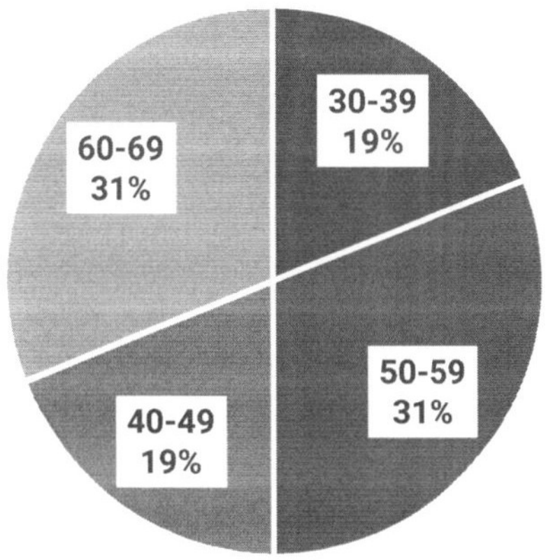

b.

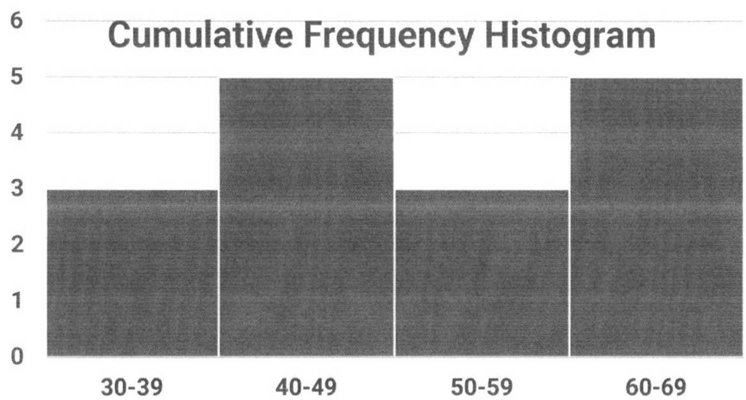

c.

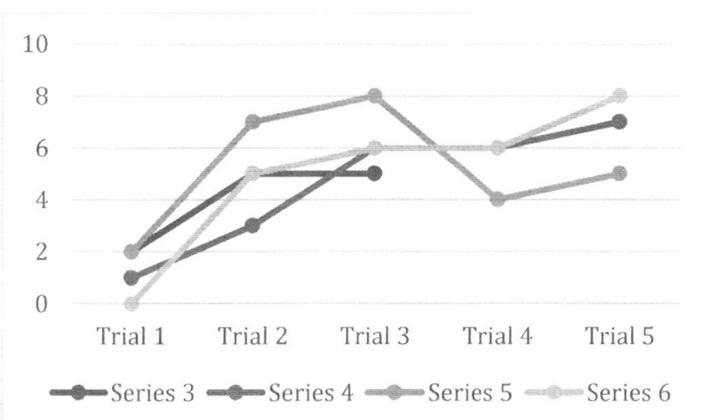

d.

37. **If $f(x) = 2x - 3$, $g(x) = x + \frac{3}{2}$, and $f(g(z)) = 6$, then what is the value of z?**

a. -3
b. 0
c. 1
d. 3

38. **In order to analyze the real estate market for two different zip codes within the city, a realtor examined the most recent 100 home sales in each zip code. She considered a house which sold within the first month of its listing to have a market time of one month; likewise, she considered a house to have a market time of two months if it sold after having been on the market for more than one month but before the end of the second month. Using this definition of market time, she determined the frequency of sales by the number of months on the market. The results are displayed below. Which of the following is a true statement for these data?**

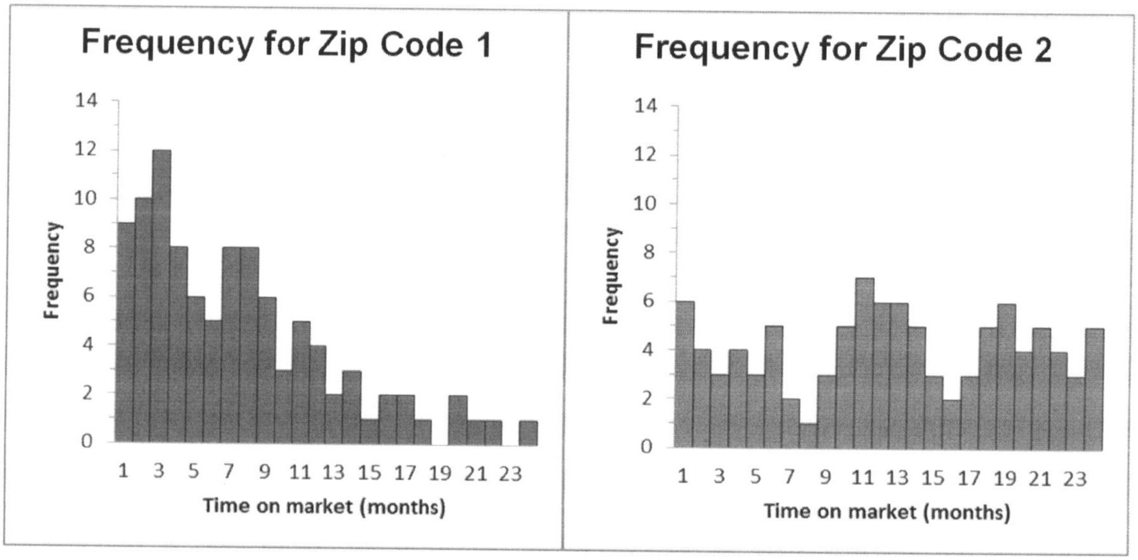

a. The median time a house spent on the market in Zip Code 1 is five months less than Zip Code 2.
b. On average, a house spent seven months longer on the market in Zip Code 2 than in Zip Code 1.
c. The mode time on the market is higher for Zip Code 1 than for Zip Code 2.
d. The median time on the market is less than the mean time on the market for Zip Code 1.

39. **If 1 inch on a map represents 10 feet and 1 yard is equal to 3 feet, how many yards apart are two points if the distance between the points on the map is 24 inches?**

a. 240 yards
b. 80 yards
c. 24 yards
d. 12 yards

40. A greenhouse is built in the shape of a square pyramid. Each of the sides of the square base measures x ft, and the height is y feet. If the height were increased by 4 ft, how much more interior space would the greenhouse have?

a. $\frac{x^2y+4x^2}{3}$ ft^3
b. $\frac{y(x^2+4)}{3}$ ft^3
c. $\frac{4x^2}{3}$ ft^3
d. 64 ft^3

41. A man invested $150 in the stock market. During the first week, he lost $45. During the second week, he tripled his money. How much does he have at the end of the second week?

a. $105
b. $210
c. $315
d. $420

42. Simplify: $\frac{2-5i}{3+2i}$

a. $-\frac{4}{13}+\frac{11}{13}i$
b. $\frac{15}{13}$
c. $-\frac{4}{13}-\frac{19}{13}i$
d. $\frac{16}{13}-\frac{19}{13}i$

43. For ΔABC, what is the length of $\overline{AB}$?

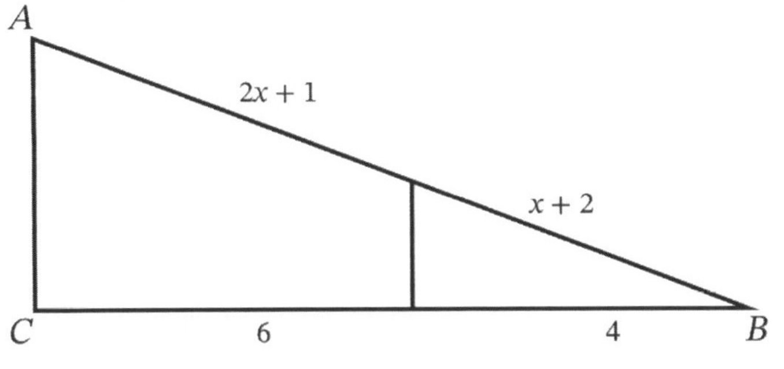

a. 4
b. 9
c. 12
d. 15

44. What is the product of the two complex numbers $6 + 5i$ and $3 - 3i$?

a. $18 - 15i$
b. $33 - 3i$
c. $33 - 9i$
d. $33 - 15i$

45. Evaluate $\lim_{x \to 2^-} \frac{|x-4|}{2-x}$.

a. -2
b. 0
c. 2
d. ∞

46. Solve the system of equations: $\begin{cases} -4x + 3y = 8 \\ 6x - 2y = -7 \end{cases}$.

a. $\left(\frac{1}{2}, \frac{10}{3}\right)$
b. $\left(-1, \frac{3}{2}\right)$
c. $\left(2, -\frac{5}{2}\right)$
d. $\left(-\frac{1}{2}, 2\right)$

Refer to the following for question 47:

The box-and-whisker plot displays student test scores assessed throughout a semester to see if students were improving.

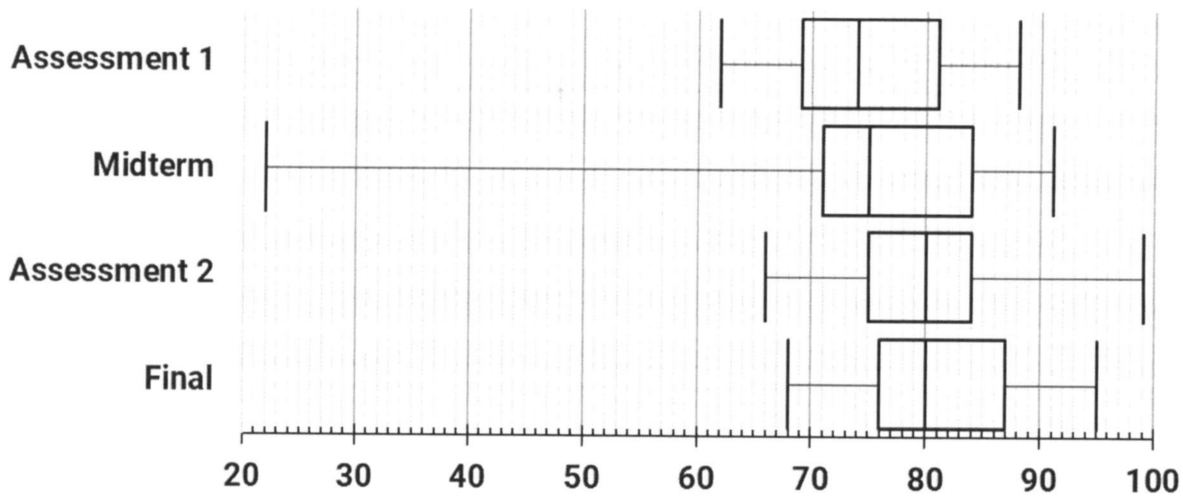

47. What is the probability that a test score chosen at random from the Final is less than 87?

a. 0.25
b. 0.5
c. 0.6
d. 0.75

48. Simplify: $\frac{(x^2y)(2xy^{-2})^3}{16x^5y^2} + \frac{3}{xy}$.

a. $\frac{3x+24y^6}{8xy^7}$

b. $\frac{x+6y^6}{2xy^7}$

c. $\frac{x+24y^5}{8xy^6}$

d. $\frac{x+6y^5}{2xy^6}$

49. The cost of admission to a theme park is shown below.

Under age 10	Ages 10–65	Over age 65
\$15	\$25	\$20

Yesterday, the theme park sold 810 tickets and earned \$14,500. There were twice as many children under 10 at the park as there were other visitors. If x, y, and z represent the number of \$15, \$25, and \$20 tickets sold, respectively, which of the following can be used to find how many of each sold?

a. $\begin{bmatrix} 1 & 1 & 1 \\ 15 & 25 & 20 \\ 1 & -2 & -2 \end{bmatrix} \begin{bmatrix} x \\ y \\ z \end{bmatrix} = \begin{bmatrix} 810 \\ 14{,}500 \\ 0 \end{bmatrix}$

b. $\begin{bmatrix} 1 & 1 & 1 \\ 15 & 25 & 20 \\ 1 & -2 & -2 \end{bmatrix} \begin{bmatrix} 810 \\ 14{,}500 \\ 0 \end{bmatrix} = \begin{bmatrix} x \\ y \\ z \end{bmatrix}$

c. $\begin{bmatrix} 1 & 15 & 1 \\ 1 & 25 & -2 \\ 1 & 20 & -2 \end{bmatrix} \begin{bmatrix} x \\ y \\ z \end{bmatrix} = \begin{bmatrix} 810 \\ 14{,}500 \\ 0 \end{bmatrix}$

d. $\begin{bmatrix} 1 & 15 & 1 \\ 1 & 25 & -2 \\ 1 & 20 & -2 \end{bmatrix} \begin{bmatrix} 810 \\ 14{,}500 \\ 0 \end{bmatrix} = \begin{bmatrix} x \\ y \\ z \end{bmatrix}$

50. A weight suspended on a spring is at its equilibrium point 6 inches above the top of a table. When the weight is pulled down 1.5 inches, it bounces above the equilibrium point and returns to the point from which it was released in 0.5 seconds. Which of these can be used to model the weight's height h above the table as a function of time t in seconds?

a. $h = -1.5\sin(2\pi t) + 6$

b. $h = -3\cos(\pi t) + 4.5$

c. $h = -1.5\cos(4\pi t) + 6$

d. $h = -3\cos(0.5\pi t) + 4.5$

Refer to the following for question 51:

The box-and-whisker plot displays a district's standardized test scores by subject.

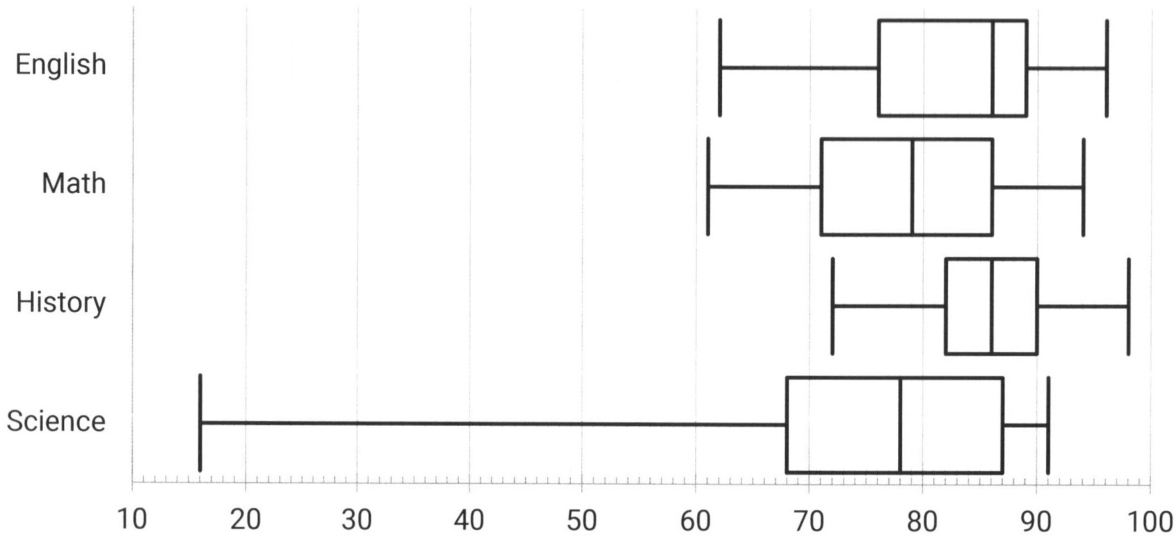

51. Which of the following statements is NOT true of the data?

a. The median better reflects student performance in Science than the mean.
b. The mean test score for English and history is the same.
c. The median of the History scores is the same as the 3rd quartile score for Math.
d. The median test score is above the mean for English.

52. A cube inscribed in a sphere has a volume of 64 cubic units. What is the volume of the sphere in cubic units?

a. $4\pi\sqrt{3}$
b. $8\pi\sqrt{3}$
c. $32\pi\sqrt{3}$
d. $256\pi\sqrt{3}$

53. Evaluate: $\lim_{x\to\infty} \frac{x^2+2x-3}{2x^2+1}$

a. -3
b. 0
c. $\frac{1}{2}$
d. ∞

Refer to the following for question 54:

Consider the following graphic showing demographics of a high school with 1,219 total students:

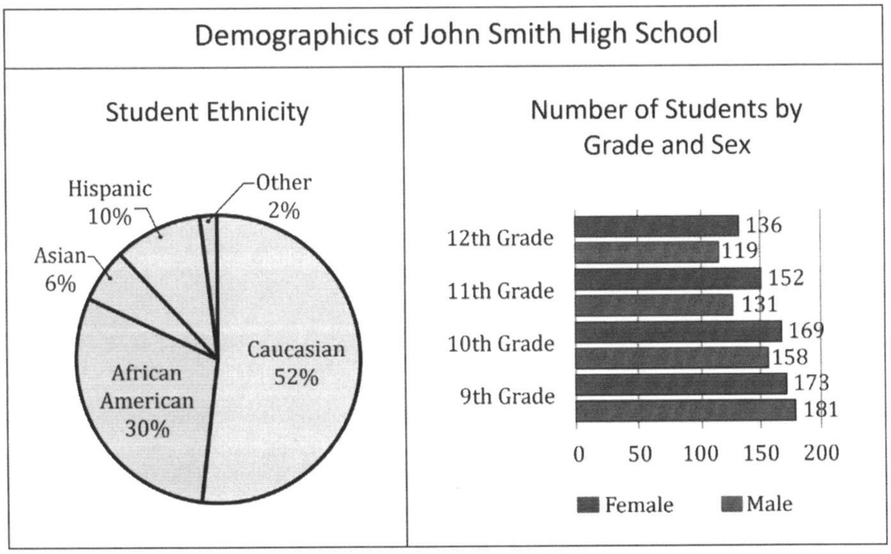

54. An eleventh grader is chosen at random to represent the school at a conference. What is the approximate probability that the student is male?

a. 0.03
b. 0.11
c. 0.22
d. 0.46

Refer to the following for question 55:

Joshua has to earn more than 92 points on the state test in order to qualify for an academic scholarship. Each question is worth 4 points, and the test has a total of 30 questions. Let x represent the number of test questions Joshua answers correctly.

55. Which of the following inequalities can be solved to determine the number of questions Joshua must answer correctly?

a. $4x < 30$
b. $4x < 92$
c. $4x > 30$
d. $4x > 92$

56. For vector $v = (0, 5)$ and vector $w = (2, 1)$, find $3(v - w)$.

a. $(6, 18)$
b. $(-6, 12)$
c. $(6, -12)$
d. $(-6, -18)$

57. Which of these defines the recursive sequence $a_1 = 2, a_{n+1} = a_n - 3$ explicitly?

a. $a_n = 2n - 3$
b. $a_n = -3n + 5$
c. $a_n = n - 1$
d. $a_n = -2n + 2$

Refer to the following for question 58:

Twenty-five children in a class are given an unevenly weighted six-sided die to see who can roll a six. Each child rolls the die twice and the teacher records how many sixes each child rolls.

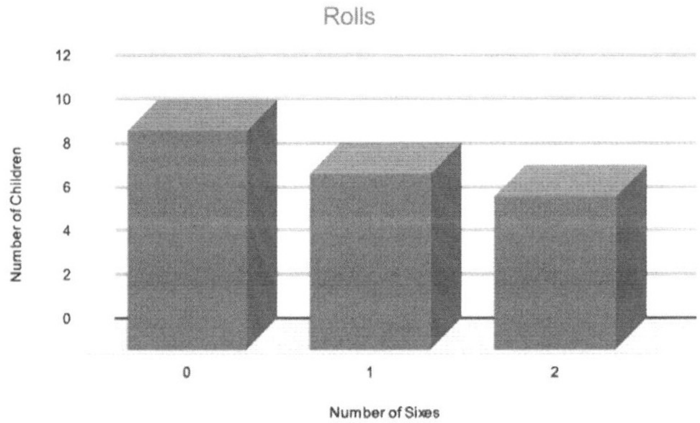

58. Given these experimental data, which of these approximates $P(\text{six})$ for a single roll of this die?

a. 0.22
b. 0.3
c. 0.44
d. 0.56

59. Simplify:

$$[2 \quad 0 \quad -5]\left(\begin{bmatrix} 4 \\ 2 \\ -1 \end{bmatrix} - \begin{bmatrix} 3 \\ 5 \\ -5 \end{bmatrix}\right)$$

a. $[-18]$
b. $\begin{bmatrix} 2 \\ 0 \\ -20 \end{bmatrix}$
c. $[2 \quad 0 \quad -20]$
d. $\begin{bmatrix} 2 & 0 & -5 \\ -6 & 0 & 15 \\ 8 & 0 & -20 \end{bmatrix}$

60. A triangle with vertices $A(-4, -3)$, $B(-2, 0)$, and $C(-1, -1)$ is reflected across $y = x - 3$ to give $\Delta A'B'C'$, which is subsequently reflected across the y-axis to give $\Delta A''B''C''$. Which of these statements is true?

a. A translation of ΔABC three units up gives $\Delta A''B''C''$.
b. A reflection of ΔABC about the x-axis gives $\Delta A''B''C''$.
c. A 90° rotation of ΔABC about $(0, -3)$ gives $\Delta A''B''C''$.
d. A 270° rotation of ΔABC about $(0, -3)$ gives $\Delta A''B''C''$.

61. Rafael has a business selling computers. He buys computers from the manufacturer for \$450 each and sells them for \$800. Each month, he must also pay fixed costs of \$3,000 for rent and utilities for his store. If he sells n computers in a month, which of the following equations can be used to find his profit?

a. $P = n(\$800 - \$450)$
b. $P = n(\$800 - \$450 - \$3{,}000)$
c. $P = \$3{,}000 \times n(\$800 - \$450)$
d. $P = n(\$800 - \$450) - \$3{,}000$

62. Solve the inequality: $|x + 6| < 9$

a. $(-15, -3)$
b. $(-15, 3)$
c. $(3, -3)$
d. $(6, -9)$

63. Solve the system of equations.

$$3x + 4y = 2$$
$$2x + 6y = -2$$

a. $\left(0, \frac{1}{2}\right)$
b. $\left(\frac{2}{5}, \frac{1}{5}\right)$
c. $(2, -1)$
d. $\left(-1, \frac{5}{4}\right)$

64. Simplify the expression $\sqrt{\frac{-54x^5}{80y^6}}$.

a. $\frac{3x^2 i\sqrt{6x}}{20y^3}$
b. $\frac{3x^2 i\sqrt{6x}}{4y^3}$
c. $\frac{-3x^2 i\sqrt{30x}}{8y^3}$
d. $\frac{3x^2 i\sqrt{30x}}{20y^3}$

65. What is the exact value of $\tan\left(-\frac{\pi}{4}\right)$?

a. -1
b. $-\frac{\sqrt{2}}{2}$
c. $\frac{\sqrt{2}}{2}$
d. 1

66. Express the area of the given triangle as a function of x.

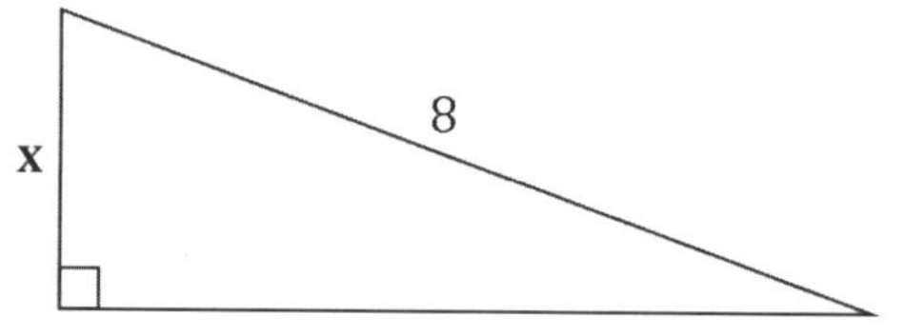

a. $A(x) = 4x$

b. $A(x) = \frac{x\sqrt{x^2-64}}{4}$

c. $A(x) = \frac{64-x^2}{2}$

d. $A(x) = \frac{x\sqrt{64-x^2}}{2}$

67. A random sample of 90 students at an elementary school were asked these three questions:

Do you like carrots?
Do you like broccoli?
Do you like cauliflower?

The results of the survey are shown below. If these data are representative of the population of students at the school, which of these is most probable?

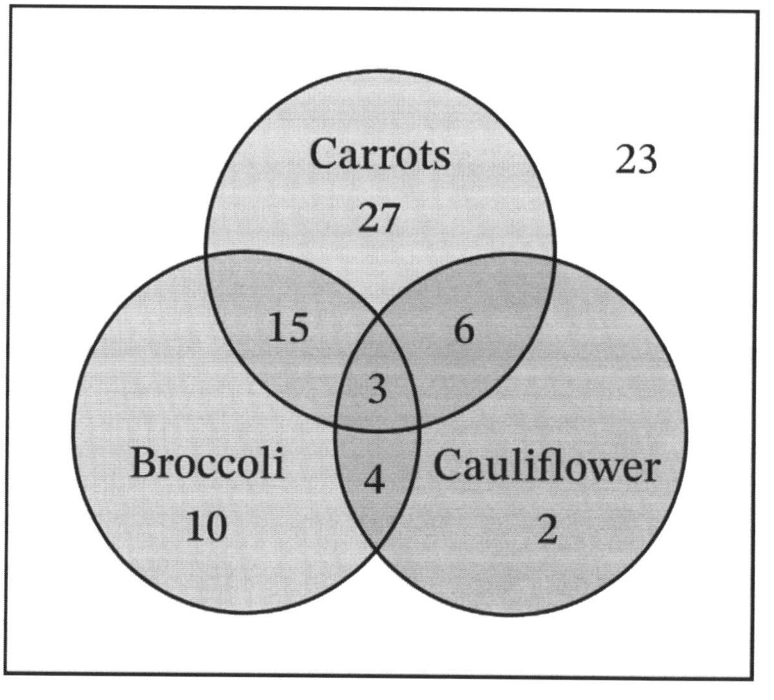

a. A student chosen at random likes broccoli.
b. Given a student chosen at random likes carrots, they will also like at least one other vegetable.
c. Given a student chosen at random likes cauliflower and broccoli, they will also like carrots.
d. A student chosen at random does not like carrots, broccoli, or cauliflower.

68. Simplify $(2 - 3i)^2 - (1 - 4i)$.

a. $\sqrt{61}$
b. $-6 - 8i$
c. $6 + 8i$
d. 10

Refer to the following for question 69:

The box-and-whisker plot displays a district's standardized test scores by subject.

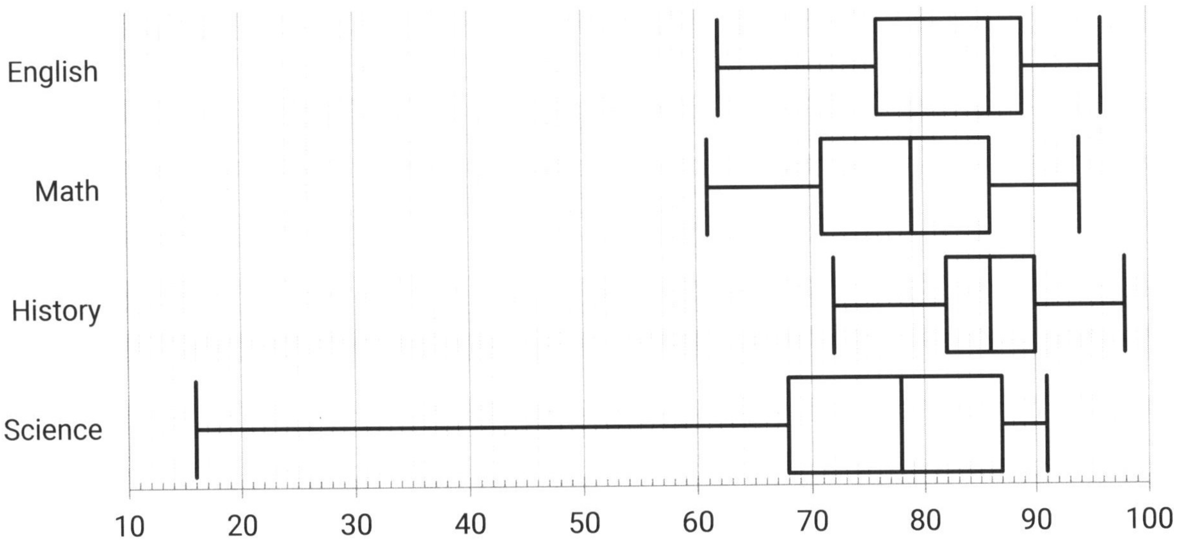

69. Which subject has the smallest range of test scores?

a. English
b. Math
c. History
d. Science

70. Which of these relationships represents y as a function of x?

a. $x = y^4$

b. 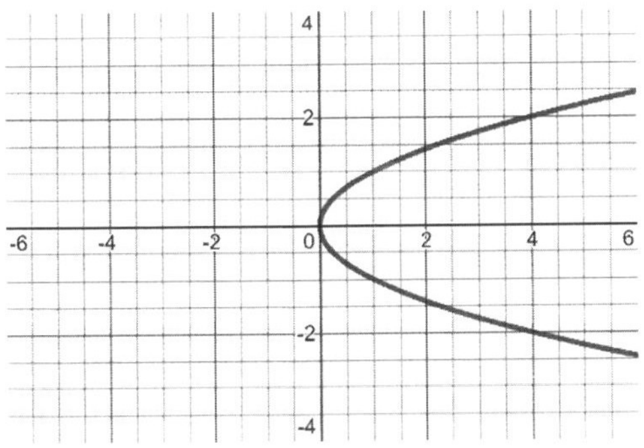

c. $y = |x - 2|$

d. 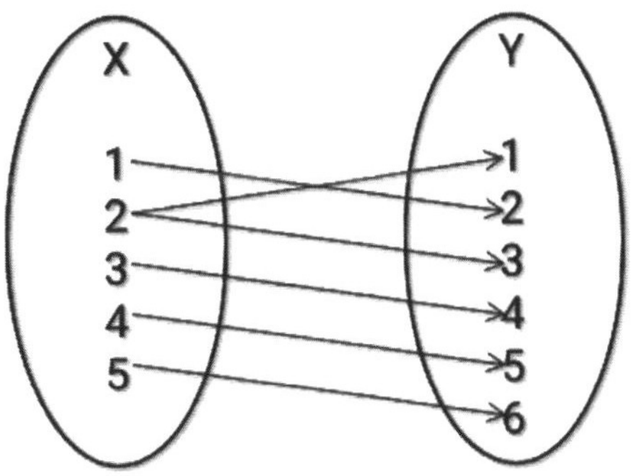

71. What is the radius of the circle defined by the equation $x^2 + y^2 - 4x + 6y - 5 = 0$?

a. $2\sqrt{3}$
b. $3\sqrt{2}$
c. $\sqrt{5}$
d. $2\sqrt{5}$

Refer to the following for question 72:

Below are graphed functions $f(x) = a_1 \sin(b_1 x)$ and $g(x) = a_2 \cos(b_2 x)$; a_1 and a_2 are integers, and b_1 and b_2 are positive rational numbers.

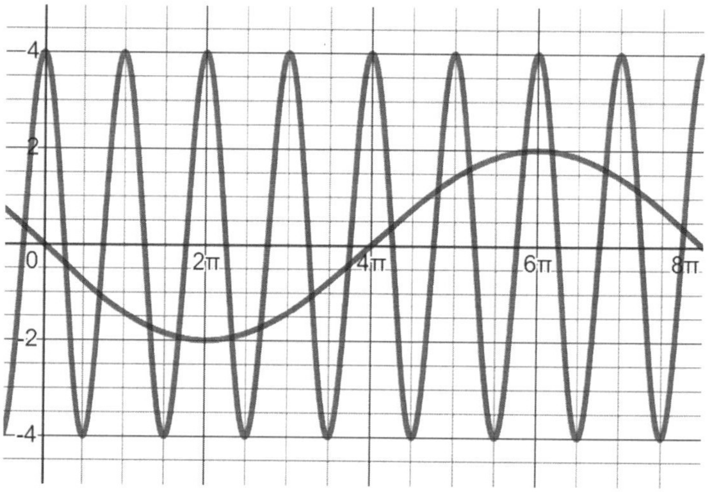

72. Which of the following statements is true?

a. $0 < a_2 < a_1$
b. $a_2 < 0 < a_1$
c. $0 < a_1 < a_2$
d. $a_1 < 0 < a_2$

73. Solve $\frac{x-2}{x-1} = \frac{x-1}{x+1} + \frac{2}{x-1}$.

a. $x = 2$
b. $x = -5$
c. $x = 1$
d. No solution

74. Two teachers from a county are chosen at random to attend a conference for high school science educators. What is the approximate probability that two women from the same department will be chosen?

	Biology	Chemistry	Physics
Women	26	31	20
Men	16	11	25

a. 8.6%
b. 10.7%
c. 11.9%
d. 13.8%

75. If $f(x) = -2x^2 - 7$, find the slope of the line tangent to the graph of $f(x)$ at $x = 1$.

a. -4
b. -2
c. 0
d. 1

76. Solve $x^4 + 9 = 10x^2$.

a. $x = \{1, 3\}$
b. $x = \{-3i, -i, i, 3i\}$
c. $x = \{i, 3i\}$
d. $x = \{-3, -1, 1, 3\}$

77. Which of these functions includes -1 as an element of the domain and -2 as an element of the range?

a. $y = \frac{1}{x-1} - 2$
b. $y = \frac{\sqrt{x-1}}{4} + 4$
c. $y = |x - 1| - 1$
d. $y = \begin{cases} x - 5 & x < -1 \\ -x + 1 & x \geq -1 \end{cases}$

78. A company is designing a paperweight in the shape of a square pyramid. Each of the sides of the square base measures x in, and the height is z in. If the length of each side of the base were increased by $\frac{1}{2}$ in, how much more volume would the paperweight have?

a. $\frac{z\left(x^2+x+\frac{z}{4}\right)}{3}$ in^3
b. $\frac{x^2z+4}{12}$ in^3
c. $\frac{z(4x+1)}{12}$ in^3
d. $\frac{1}{4}$ in^3

79. Attending a summer camp are 12 six-year-olds, 15 seven-year-olds, 14 eight-year-olds, 12 nine-year-olds, and 10 ten-year-olds. If a camper is randomly selected to participate in a special event, what is the probability that he or she is at least eight years old?

a. $\frac{2}{9}$
b. $\frac{22}{63}$
c. $\frac{4}{7}$
d. $\frac{3}{7}$

80. Angles m and n are acute angles (measured in degrees) in two different triangles. The sine of m is equal to the cosine of n. If $m = 3x + 12$ and $n = -x + 32$, what is x?

a. 5
b. 9
c. 23
d. 81

81. Given the figure and the following information, find the length of $\overline{DE}$ to the nearest tenth.

$\overline{AD}$ is an altitude of ΔABC
$\overline{DE}$ is an altitude of triangle ΔADC
$\overline{BD} \cong \overline{DC}$
$\overline{BC} = 24; \overline{AD} = 5$

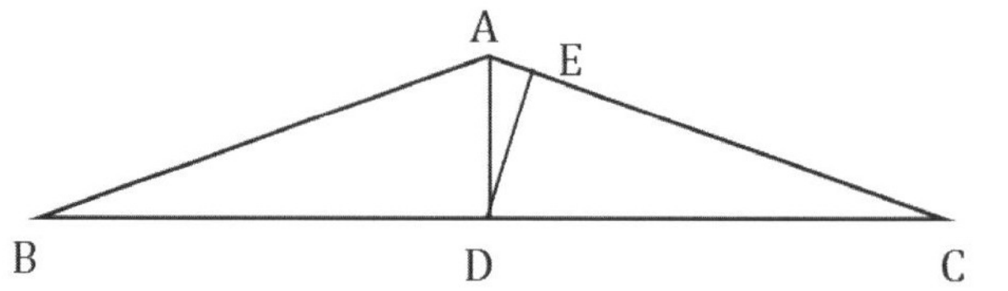

a. 4.2
b. 4.6
c. 4.9
d. 5.4

82. Which of the following is equivalent to $2 - \frac{1}{2}x < 1$?

a. $x < 2$
b. $x > 2$
c. $x < -2$
d. $x > -2$

83. Find the area of the finite region between the graphs of $y = x - 2$ and $y = x^2 - 2x - 12$.

a. $\frac{343}{6}$
b. 18
c. $\frac{45}{2}$
d. 25

84. Simplify the following: $\frac{x^2}{y^2} + \frac{x}{y^3}$

a. $\frac{x^3+x}{y^3}$
b. $\frac{x^2+xy}{y^3}$
c. $\frac{x^2y+xy}{y^3}$
d. $\frac{x^2y+x}{y^3}$

85. A ball is tossed straight up. Its path can be modeled by the first-quadrant graph of the equation $h(t) = -16t^2 + 56t + 6$, where h is the height of the ball in feet and t is the time in seconds after the ball is thrown. What is the average rate of change in the ball's height with respect to time over the interval $[2, 3]$?

a. -30 ft/s
b. -24 ft/s
c. 30 ft/s
d. 84 ft/s

86. The heights of 200 high school males are normally distributed with a mean height of 67.5 inches and a standard deviation of 3.5 inches. In a normal distribution, approximately 68% of values are within one standard deviation of the mean. About how many individuals from the selected group are shorter than 5'11"?

a. 125
b. 142
c. 168
d. 184

87. Roxana walks x meters west and $x + 20$ meters south to get to her friend's house. On a neighborhood map which has a scale of 1 cm : 10 m, the direct distance between Roxana's house and her friend's house is 10 cm. How far did Roxana walk to her friend's house?

a. 60 m
b. 80 m
c. 100 m
d. 140 m

88. Calculate $\int \left(6x^2 + \frac{1}{2}x - 3\right) dx$.

a. $x^3 + x^2 - 3x + C$
b. $12x^3 + x^2 - 3x + C$
c. $2x^3 + \frac{1}{4}x^2 - 3x + C$
d. $12x^2 + x + C$

89. The two shortest sides of a right triangle are 6 and 8 units long, respectively. What is the perimeter of the triangle?

a. 10 units
b. 14 units
c. 18 units
d. 24 units

90. Solve $3x^2 + 6x = -4$.

a. $x = \frac{-3 \pm i\sqrt{3}}{3}$
b. $x = -1 \pm i\sqrt{3}$
c. $x = \pm\frac{i\sqrt{3}}{3}$
d. $x = \frac{-3 \pm i\sqrt{3}}{6}$

Answer Key and Explanations for Test #1

1. A: To solve, first figure out how much space remains once her car is in the garage. 19 feet − 15 feet = 4 feet. To center the car, she should park halfway between the remaining space. Therefore, her car would need to be parked 2 feet from the front of the garage for it to be centered.

2. C: Find the missing angle measures in the diagram by using angle and triangle properties. Then, use the law of sines to find the distance y between the window and the wife's car: $\frac{60}{\sin 15°} = \frac{y}{\sin 45°}$, so $y = \frac{60 \sin 45°}{\sin 15°} \approx 163.9$ ft. Use this number in a sine or cosine function to find x: $\sin 30° \approx \frac{x}{163.9}$, so $x \approx 163.9 \sin 30° \approx 82$. Therefore, the man's wife is parked approximately 82 feet from the building.

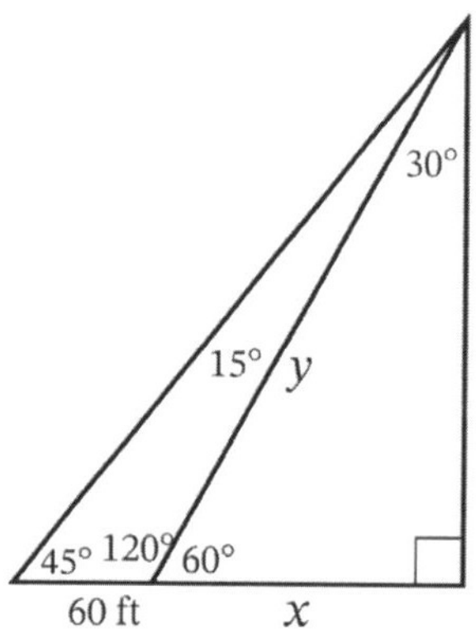

Alternatively, notice that when the man is looking down at a 45-degree angle, the triangle that is formed is an isosceles triangle, meaning that the height of his office is the same as the distance from the office to his car, or $x + 60$ feet. With this knowledge, the problem can be modeled with a single equation.

$$\frac{x+60}{x} = \tan 60°$$
$$x + 60 = x \tan 60°$$
$$60 = x \tan 60° - x$$
$$60 = x(\tan 60° - 1)$$
$$\frac{60}{\tan 60° - 1} = x$$
$$82 \approx x$$

With both methods of solving, the wife's car is approximately 82 feet from the building.

3. B: The acceleration a of an object at time t is the derivative of the velocity v of the object with respect to time t. Velocity of the object is the derivative of the position s of the object with respect to time t. So, given the velocity of an object at time t, $s(t)$ can be found by taking the integral of the $v(t)$, and $a(t)$ can be found by taking the derivative of $v(t)$.

$$\begin{aligned} s(t) &= \int v(t)dt \\ &= \int (-t^2 + 8t)dt \\ &= -\frac{1}{3}t^3 + 4t^2 + C \end{aligned}$$

Since the position of the car at time 0 is 0:

$$\begin{aligned} 0 &= s(0) \\ 0 &= 4(0)^2 - \frac{1}{3}(0)^3 + C \\ 0 &= 0 - 0 + C \\ 0 &= C \end{aligned}$$

Therefore, $s(t) = -\frac{1}{3}t^3 + 4t^2$.

The acceleration at time t is: $a(t) = v'(t) = -2t + 8$.

Find the time at which the acceleration is equal to 0.

$$\begin{aligned} 0 &= 8 - 2t \\ t &= 4 \end{aligned}$$

Then, find $s(4)$ to find the position of the car when the velocity is 0.

$$\begin{aligned} s(t) &= -\frac{1}{3}t^3 + 4t^2 \\ s(4) &= -\frac{1}{3}(4)^3 + 4(4)^2 \\ s(4) &= -\frac{64}{3} + 64 \\ s(4) &= \frac{128}{3} \end{aligned}$$

Therefore, the position of the car when its acceleration is 0 is $\frac{128}{3}$.

4. C: If l and w represent the length and width of the enclosed area, its perimeter is equal to $2l + 2w$; since the fence is positioned x feet from the lot's edges on each side, the perimeter of the lot is $2(l + 2x) + 2(w + 2x)$. Since the amount of money saved by fencing the smaller area is $432, and since the fencing material costs $12 per linear foot, 36 fewer feet of material are used to fence around the playground than would have been used to fence around the lot. This can be expressed as the following equation.

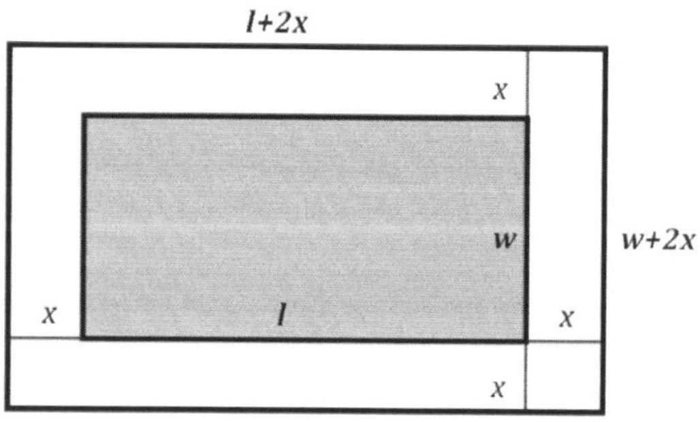

$$2(l + 2x) + 2(w + 2x) - (2l + 2w) = 36$$
$$2l + 4x + 2w + 4x - 2l - 2w = 36$$
$$8x = 36$$
$$x = 4.5 \text{ ft}$$

The difference in the area of the lot and the enclosed space is 141 yd^2, which is the same as 1,269 ft^2. So, $(l + 2x)(w + 2x) - lw = 1{,}269$. Substituting 4.5 for x, we get the following equation that we can solve for $l + w$.

$$(l + 9)(w + 9) - lw = 1{,}269$$
$$lw + 9l + 9w + 81 - lw = 1{,}269$$
$$9l + 9w = 1{,}188$$
$$9(l + w) = 1{,}188$$
$$l + w = 132 \text{ ft}$$

Therefore, the perimeter of the enclosed space, $2(l + w)$, is $2(132) = 264$ ft. The cost of 264 ft of fencing is $264 \times \$12 = \$3{,}168$.

5. B: The population is approximately 6,000, so 80% of the population consists of about 4,800 individuals over age 10. Ten percent of 4,800 is 480, the approximate number of students in the local high school. Since there are four grades, there are about 120 students in each grade. So, the number of 11th graders is likely between 100 and 150.

6. C: The expression representing the charge for Ride Service A is $\$10 + \$0.25(m - 10)$, where m is the number of miles. Set this expression equal to the charge for Ride Service B, which is $\$0.40m$. Solve for m to find the number of miles the two companies charge the same amount.

$$\$10 + \$0.25(m - 10) = \$0.40m$$
$$\$10 + \$0.25m - \$2.50 = \$0.40m$$
$$\$7.50 = \$0.15m$$
$$m = 50$$

So, the cost of the two services would be the same for a 50-mile ride.

7. A: The composition function $(g \circ f)(x)$ can be rewritten as $g(f(x))$. This means that anywhere there is an x in the function $g(x)$, it should be replaced with $2x + 4$. After substituting, simplify the expression.

$$\begin{aligned} g(2x+4) &= (2x+4)^2 - 3(2x+4) + 2 \\ &= 4x^2 + 16x + 16 - 6x - 12 + 2 \\ &= 4x^2 + 10x + 6 \end{aligned}$$

8. C: Using rectangles with a width of 1, we can find the left and right Riemann sums to approximate the area under the curve.

The left Riemann sum: $20 + 25 + 28 + 30 + 29 + 26 + 22 + 16 + 12 + 10 + 10 + 13 = 241$

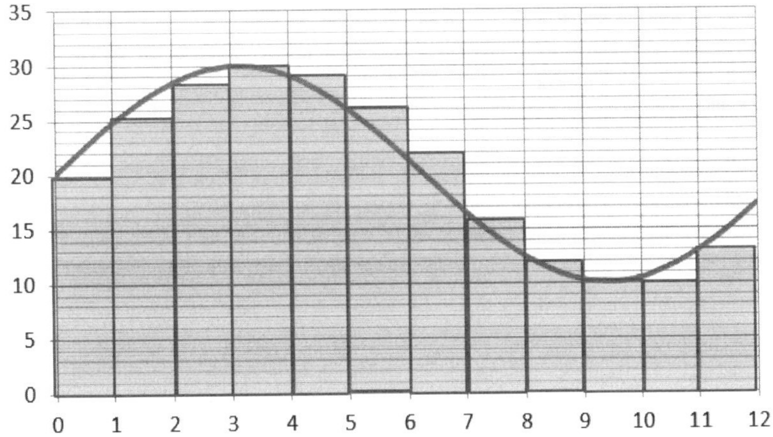

The right Riemann sum: $25 + 28 + 30 + 29 + 26 + 22 + 16 + 12 + 10 + 10 + 13 + 17 = 238$

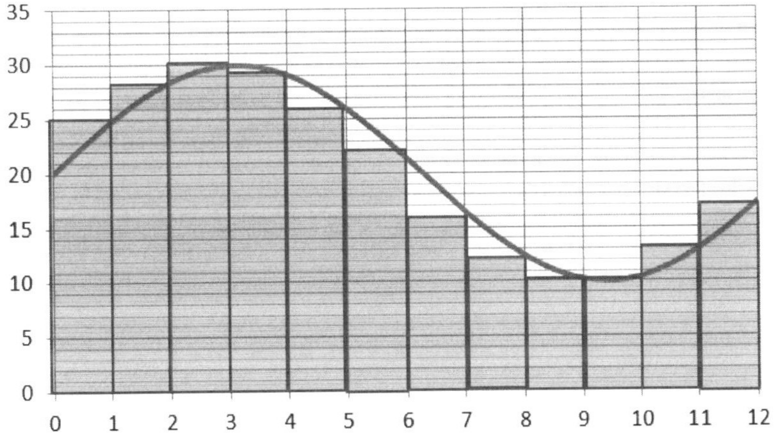

Thus, the bounds on A are: $238 < A < 241$.

9. B: The trigonometric identity $1 + \cot^2\theta = \csc^2\theta$ can be used to rewrite $\csc^2\theta = 2\cot\theta$ as $1 + \cot^2\theta = 2\cot\theta$. Now, set the equation equal to 0 to get $\cot^2\theta - 2\cot\theta + 1 = 0$. Solve by factoring.

$$\begin{aligned} \cot^2\theta - 2\cot\theta + 1 &= 0 \\ (\cot\theta - 1)^2 &= 0 \\ \cot\theta - 1 &= 0 \\ \cot\theta &= 1 \end{aligned}$$

Thus, from the unit circle, for $0 < \theta \leq 2\pi$, $\cot\theta = 1$ when $\theta = \frac{\pi}{4}$ or $\frac{5\pi}{4}$.

10. B: Euclidean geometry is based on the flat plane. One of Euclid's five axioms, from which all Euclidean geometric theorems are derived, is the parallel postulate, which states that in a plane, for any line l and point A not on l, exactly one line which passes through A does not intersect l.

Non-Euclidean geometry considers lines on surfaces that are not flat. For instance, on the Earth's surface, if point A represents the North Pole and line l represents the equator (which does not pass through A), all lines of longitude pass through point A and intersect line l. In elliptical geometry, there are infinitely many lines which pass though A and intersect l, and there is no line which passes through A which does not also intersect l. In hyperbolic geometry when A is not on l, many lines which pass through A diverge from l, or put more succinctly, at least two lines that go through A do not intersect l.

11. D: There are many ways Josephine may have applied her knowledge to determine how to approximately measure her medicine using her plastic spoon. The expression below shows how she converts from cubic centimeters to spoons.

$$25\text{ cc} \times \frac{1\text{ mL}}{1\text{ cc}} \times \frac{1\text{L}}{1{,}000\text{ mL}} \times \frac{0.5\text{ gal}}{2\text{ L}} \times \frac{16\text{ c}}{1\text{ gal}} \times \frac{48\text{ t}}{1\text{ c}} \times \frac{1\text{ spoonful}}{1\text{ t}}$$

$$\frac{25}{1{,}000} \times \frac{1}{4} \times 16 \times 48$$

The only choice which correctly uses dimensional analysis is choice D.

12. B: Bacterial growth is exponential. Let x be the number of doubling times and a be the number of bacteria in the colony originally and y be the number of bacteria after a doubling times. After 30 minutes the population would have doubled two times.

$$\begin{aligned} a(2^x) &= y \\ a(2^2) &= 4 \times 10^3 \\ 4a &= 4 \times 10^3 \\ a &= 10^3 \end{aligned}$$

The equation for determining the number of bacteria is $y = (2^x) \times 10^3$. Since the bacteria double every 15 minutes, they go through four doubling times every hour. So, when the bacteria are allowed to grow for six hours, they will have gone through 24 doubling times. When $x = 24$, $y = (2^{24}) \times 10^3 = 16{,}777{,}216 \times 10^3$, which is approximately 1.7×10^{10}.

13. C: Combine the first two equations to eliminate z.

$$\begin{array}{rrrrcr} & 3x & +4y & -z & = & 5 \\ + & -x & +2y & +z & = & 0 \\ \hline & 2x & +6y & & = & 5 \end{array}$$

Multiply the original second equation by –2 and combine it with the third equation to eliminate z.

$$\begin{array}{rrrrcr} & 2x & -4y & -2z & = & 0 \\ + & x & +2y & +2z & = & 2 \\ \hline & 3x & -2y & & = & 2 \end{array}$$

Multiply the equation from step two by 3 and combine to eliminate y.

$$\begin{array}{rrrrcr} & 2x & + & 6y & = & 5 \\ + & 9x & - & 6y & = & 6 \\ \hline & 11x & & & = & 11 \\ & x & & & = & 1 \end{array}$$

Substitute 1 for x in the equation from step 2 to find y.

$$\begin{aligned} 3(1) - 2y &= 2 \\ -2y &= -1 \\ y &= \frac{1}{2} \end{aligned}$$

Substitute 1 for x and $\frac{1}{2}$ for y into the second original equation to find z.

$$\begin{aligned} -1 + 2\left(\frac{1}{2}\right) + z &= 0 \\ -1 + 1 + z &= 0 \\ z &= 0 \end{aligned}$$

Therefore, the solution to the system of equations is $\left(1, \frac{1}{2}, 0\right)$.

14. B: Use trigonometric identities to simplify. First, convert $\sec\theta$ to $\frac{1}{\cos\theta}$.

$$\sin\theta\sec\theta$$

$$\sin\theta \times \frac{1}{\cos\theta}$$

Then, multiply the two values.

$$\frac{\sin\theta}{\cos\theta}$$

Remember, $\frac{\sin\theta}{\cos\theta} = \tan\theta$, so the simplified form of the expression is $\tan\theta$.

15. C: All regular polygons have rotational symmetry. The angle of rotation is the smallest angle by which the polygon can be rotated such that it maps onto itself. Any multiple of this angle will also map the polygon onto itself. The angle of rotation for a regular polygon is the angle formed between two lines drawn from consecutives vertices to the center of the polygon. Since the vertices of a regular polygon lie on a circle, for a regular polygon with n sides, the angle of rotation measures $\frac{360°}{n}$.

Number of sides of regular polygon	Angle of rotation	Angles ≤ 360° which map the polygon onto itself
4	$\frac{360}{4} = 90°$	90°, 180°, 270°, 360°
6	$\frac{360}{6} = 60°$	60°, 120°, 180°, 240°, 300°, 360°
8	$\frac{360}{8} = 45°$	45°, 90°, 135°, 180°, 225°, 270°, 315°, 360°
10	$\frac{360}{10} = 36°$	36°, 72°, 108°, 144°, 180°, 216°, 252°, 288°, 324°, 360°

16. C: If $f(x) = 10^x$ and $f(x) = 5$, then $5 = 10^x$. Write this in the form of a logarithm, $\log_{10}5 = x$. Now, use a calculator to find that $x \approx 0.7$.

17. C: On the unit circle, $\sin\theta = \frac{\sqrt{3}}{2}$ when $\theta = \frac{\pi}{3}$ and when $\theta = \frac{2\pi}{3}$. Since only $\frac{2\pi}{3}$ is in the given range of $\frac{\pi}{2} < \theta < \pi$, $\theta = \frac{2\pi}{3}$.

18. A: The given values make the Pythagorean theorem true, that is $5^2 + 12^2 = 13^2$. So, this is a right triangle. Let the base of the triangle be $5x$ and the height of the triangle be $12x$. So, the area is $A = \frac{1}{2}bh$, or $\frac{1}{2}(5x)(12x) = 30x^2$.

19. A: "A square root of twice the sum of x and 6 is equal to half of x" is represented by the equation $\sqrt{2(x+6)} = \frac{1}{2}x$. Solve for x.

$$\sqrt{2(x+6)} = \frac{1}{2}x$$
$$\sqrt{2x+12} = \frac{1}{2}x$$
$$\left(\sqrt{2x+12}\right)^2 = \left(\frac{1}{2}x\right)^2$$
$$2x + 12 = \frac{1}{4}x^2$$
$$4(2x+12) = x^2$$
$$8x + 48 = x^2$$
$$x^2 - 8x - 48 = 0$$
$$(x+4)(x-12) = 0$$
$$x = -4, 12$$

There is not an answer choice of, "no solution." So, there is no need to check your answer in the original equation. 12 must be a possible value of x.

20. C: The definition of the derivative of f at 1, or $f'(1)$, is the limit of the difference quotient $\lim_{h\to 0}\frac{f(1+h)-f(1)}{h}$. Rather than find the limit, evaluate the derivative of the function at $x = 1$.

$$f(x) = 3x^3 - x^2 + \frac{1}{2}$$
$$f'(x) = 9x^2 - 2x$$
$$f'(1) = 9(1)^2 - 2(1) = 9 - 2 = 7$$

21. A: The area of a circle is πr^2, so the area of a semicircle is $\frac{\pi r^2}{2}$. Illustrated below is a method that can be used to find the area of the shaded region.

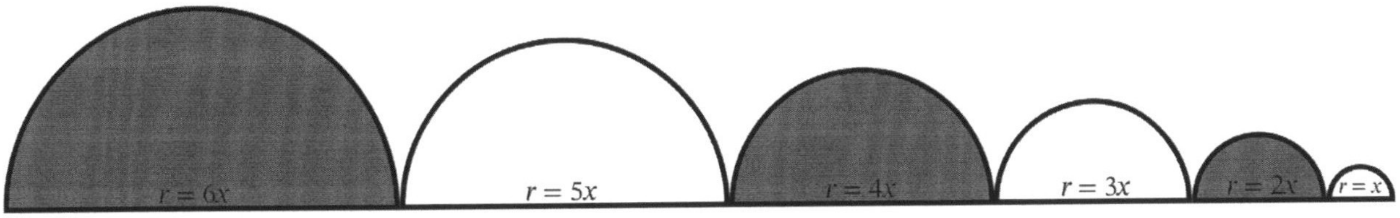

$$\begin{aligned} A &= \frac{\pi(6x)^2}{2} - \frac{\pi(5x)^2}{2} + \frac{\pi(4x)^2}{2} - \frac{\pi(3x)^2}{2} + \frac{\pi(2x)^2}{2} - \frac{\pi(x)^2}{2} \\ &= \frac{36\pi x^2}{2} - \frac{25\pi x^2}{2} + \frac{16\pi x^2}{2} - \frac{9\pi x^2}{2} + \frac{4\pi x^2}{2} - \frac{\pi x^2}{2} \\ &= \frac{(36 - 25 + 16 - 9 + 4 - 1)\pi x^2}{2} \\ &= \frac{21\pi x^2}{2} \end{aligned}$$

22. C: Sketch a diagram (this one is not to scale) and label the known segments. Because $\overline{CD}$ is bisected, the point of tangency divides the segment into two pieces measuring 4 and 4. From here, use the property that two segments are congruent when they originate from the same point outside of a circle and are both tangent to the circle. The point of tangency of $\overline{BC}$ divides the segment into two pieces measuring 4 and 6; the point of tangency of $\overline{AB}$ divides the segment into two pieces measuring 6 and 8; the point of tangency of $\overline{AD}$ divides the segment into two pieces measuring 8 and 4. Therefore $\overline{AD} = 8 + 4 = 12$.

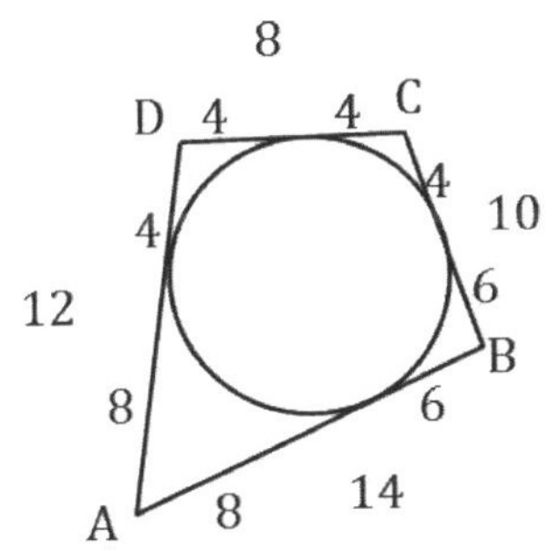

23. A: The line with fewer oscillations represents the sine function, $f(x)$, and the line with more oscillations represents a cosine function, $g(x)$. The amplitude of $f(x)$ is 2, and the amplitude of $g(x)$ is 4. The function $y = \sin x$ has a period of 2π, while the graph of function $f(x) = a_1 \sin(b_1 x)$

has a period of 8π; therefore, $b_1 = \frac{2\pi}{8\pi} = 0.25$. The graph of $g(x) = a_2 \cos(b_2 x)$ has a period of $\frac{8\pi}{8} = \pi$, so $b_2 = \frac{2\pi}{\pi} = 2$, which is not between 0 and 1.

24. C: If there is one white petunia for every three red petunias, we can write that red petunias = 3(white petunias). We can then substitute 8 for the white petunias and r for the red petunias: $r = 3(8)$. We look through the answer choices to see which matches this. Answer choice A can be rewritten as $r = \frac{8}{3}$. Answer choice B can be rewritten as $r = \frac{3}{8}$. Answer choice C can be rewritten as $r = 3(8)$. Answer choice D can be rewritten as $r = 8 - 3$. So only answer choice C matches.

25. C: The expression representing the monthly charge for Company A is $\$25 + \$0.05m$, where m is the time in minutes spent talking on the phone. Set this expression equal to the monthly charge for Company B, which is \$50. Solve for m to find the number of minutes the two companies charge the same amount.

$$\begin{aligned} \$25 + \$0.05m &= \$50 \\ \$0.05m &= \$25 \\ m &= 500 \end{aligned}$$

Notice that the answer choices are given in hours, not in minutes. Since there are 60 minutes in an hour, $m = \frac{500}{60}$ hours $= 8\frac{1}{3}$ hours. One-third of an hour is 20 minutes, so m is 8 hours and 20 minutes.

26. B: The manufacturer wishes to minimize the surface area A of the can while keeping its volume V fixed at $0.5\text{ L} = 500\text{ mL} = 500\text{ cm}^3$. The formula for the surface area of a cylinder is $A = 2\pi rh + 2\pi r^2$, and the formula for volume is $V = \pi r^2 h$. To combine the two formulas into one, solve the volume formula for r or h and substitute the resulting expression into the surface area formula for r or h. The volume of the cylinder is 500 cm^3, so $500 = \pi r^2 h$ becomes $h = \frac{500}{\pi r^2}$. Therefore, $A = 2\pi rh + 2\pi r^2$ becomes $2\pi r\left(\frac{500}{\pi r^2}\right) + 2\pi r^2 = \frac{1{,}000}{r} + 2\pi r^2$. Find the critical point(s) by setting the first derivative equal to zero and solving for r. Note that r represents the radius of the can and must therefore be a positive number.

$$\begin{aligned} A &= 1{,}000r^{-1} + 2\pi r^2 \\ A' &= -1{,}000r^{-2} + 4\pi r \\ 0 &= -\frac{1{,}000}{r^2} + 4\pi r \\ \frac{1{,}000}{r^2} &= 4\pi r \\ 1{,}000 &= 4\pi r^3 \\ \sqrt[3]{\frac{1{,}000}{4\pi}} &= r \\ r &\approx 4.3\text{ cm} \end{aligned}$$

So, when $r \approx 4.3$ cm, the minimum surface area is obtained. When the radius of the can is 4.3 cm, its height is $h \approx \frac{500}{\pi(4.3)^2} \approx 8.6$ cm, and surface area is approximately $\frac{1{,}000}{4.3} + 2\pi(4.3)^2 \approx 348.73\text{ cm}^2$.

Confirm that the surface area is greater when the radius is slightly smaller or larger than 4.3 cm. For instance, when $r = 4$ cm, the surface area is approximately 350.5 cm^2, and when $r = 4.5$ cm, the surface area is approximately 349.5 cm^2.

27. D: The sequence $\frac{1}{3}, \frac{1}{9}, \frac{1}{27}, \frac{1}{81}, \ldots$ may be used to represent the situation. Substituting the initial value of $\frac{1}{3}$ and common ratio of $\frac{1}{3}$ into the formula $S = \frac{a}{1-r}$ gives $\frac{\frac{1}{3}}{1-\frac{1}{3}}$, which simplifies to $S = \frac{\frac{1}{3}}{\frac{2}{3}}$ or $S = \frac{1}{2}$.

28. B: If $f(x) = x + 3$, then $f(g(x)) = g(x) + 3$ and $g(f(x)) = g(x + 3)$. We are asked for which of these possibilities of $g(x)$ is it true that $g(x) + 3 = g(x + 3)$. The only one for which this is true is $g(x) = x - 4$: $g(x) + 3 = (x - 4) + 3 = x - 1$, and $g(x + 3) = (x + 3) - 4 = x - 1$. Since $x - 1 = x - 1$, the condition is satisfied. In contrast if we try, for example, choice A, $g(x) = -x$, we get $g(x) + 3 = (-x) + 3 = -x + 3$, and $g(x + 3) = -(x + 3) = -x - 3$; $-x + 3 \neq -x - 3$, so this does not satisfy the condition of the problem. The other choices also do not result in a true statement.

29. C: To find the derivative, use the chain rule $\left(\frac{dy}{dx} = \frac{dy}{du} \times \frac{du}{dx}\right)$.

$$y = e^{x^3 - x}$$

Let $u = x^3 - x$ and find $\frac{du}{dx}$.

$$\frac{du}{dx} = 3x^2 - 1$$

Then, let $y = e^u$ and find $\frac{dy}{du}$.

$$\frac{dy}{du} = e^u$$

Finally, combine the two using the chain rule.

$$\frac{dy}{dx} = (e^{x^3 - x}) \times (3x^2 - 1) = (3x^2 - 1)e^{x^3 - x}$$

30. B: In order for a set to be a group under operation $*$:

- The set must be closed under that operation. In other words, when the operation is performed on any two members of the set, the result must also be a member of that set.
- The set must demonstrate associativity under the operation: $a * (b * c) = (a * b) * c$.
- There must exist an identity element e in the group: $a * e = e * a = a$.
- For every element in the group, there must exist an inverse element in the group: $a * b = b * a = e$.

Choice A can be eliminated as the correct answer because the set $\{-i, 0, i\}$ does not contain the multiplicative identity 1. Though choices C and D contain the element 1, neither is closed: for example, since $i \times i = -1$, –1 must be an element of the group. Choice B is closed, contains the multiplicative identity 1, and the inverse of each element is included in the set as well. Of course, multiplication is an associative operation, so the set $\{-1, 1, i, -i\}$ forms a group under multiplication.

$\times$	$-\mathbf{1}$	$\mathbf{1}$	$\boldsymbol{i}$	$-\boldsymbol{i}$
$-\mathbf{1}$	1	-1	$-i$	i
$\mathbf{1}$	-1	1	i	$-i$
$\boldsymbol{i}$	$-i$	i	-1	1
$-\boldsymbol{i}$	i	$-i$	1	-1

31. B: The vertex form of a quadratic equation is $y = a(x - h)^2 + k$, where $x = h$ is the parabola's axis of symmetry and (h, k) is the parabola's vertex. The vertex of the graph is $(1,2)$, so the equation can be written as $y = a(x - 1)^2 + 2$. The parabola passes through the point $(0,1)$, so $1 = a(0 - 1)^2 + 2$. Solve for a:

$$\begin{aligned} 1 &= a(0 - 1)^2 + 2 \\ 1 &= a + 2 \\ -1 &= a \end{aligned}$$

So, the vertex form of the parabola is $y = -(x - 1)^2 + 2$. Write the equation in standard form: $y = ax^2 + bx + c$.

$$\begin{aligned} y &= -(x - 1)^2 + 2 \\ y &= -(x - 1)(x - 1) + 2 \\ y &= -(x^2 - 2x + 1) + 2 \\ y &= -x^2 + 2x - 1 + 2 \\ y &= -x^2 + 2x + 1 \end{aligned}$$

32. C: 52% of the student population is Caucasian. There are 630 female students at the school out of 1,219 students, so the percentage of female students is $\frac{630}{1{,}219} \times 100\% \approx 52\%$. The percentages, rounded to the nearest whole number, are the same.

33. C: When the dress is marked down by 20%, the cost of the dress is 80% of its original price. Since a percentage can be written as a fraction by placing the percentage over 100, the reduced price of the dress can be written as $\frac{80}{100}x$, or $\frac{4}{5}x$, where x is the original price. When discounted an extra 25%, the dress costs 75% of the reduced price. This results in the expression $\frac{75}{100}\left(\frac{4}{5}x\right)$, which can be simplified to $\frac{3}{4}\left(\frac{4}{5}x\right)$, or $\frac{3}{5}x$. So the final price of the dress is three-fifths of the original price.

34. B: First, use the properties of logarithms to solve for y:

$3\log_3 y + \log_3 3 = 4$	Write out the equation given.
$\log_3 y^3 + \log_3 3 = 4$	Rewrite the first term using the power rule of logarithms: $p \cdot \log_b m = \log_b m^p$.
$\log_3 3y^3 = 4$	Rewrite the left side using the product rule of logarithms: $\log_b m + \log_b n = \log_b mn$.
$3y^3 = 3^4$	Rewrite the logarithmic equation as an exponential equation.
$3y^3 = 81$	Simplify the right side.
$y^3 = 27$	Divide both sides by 3.
$y = 3$	Take the cube root of both sides.

Finally, substitute 3 for y in the expression $\log_y 243$ and simplify: $\log_3 243 = 5$ since $3^5 = 243$.

35. D: By definition, when $f(x)$ and $g(x)$ are inverse functions, $f(g(x)) = g(f(x)) = x$. So, $f(g(4)) = 4$.

36. A: To draw a box-and-whisker plot from the data, find the median, quartiles, and upper and lower limits. The median is $\frac{47+52}{2} = 49.5$, the lower quartile is $\frac{41+43}{2} = 42$, and the upper quartile is $\frac{60+65}{2} = 62.5$. The box of the box-and-whisker plot goes through the quartiles, and a line through the box represents the median of the data. The whiskers extend from the box to the lower and upper limits, unless there are any outliers in the set. In this case, there are no outliers, so the box-and-whisker plot in choice A correctly represents the data set.

To draw a pie chart, find the percentage of data contained in each of the ranges shown. There are 3 out of 16 numbers between 30 and 39, inclusive, so the percentage shown in the pie chart for that range of data is $\frac{3}{16} \times 100\% \approx 19\%$; there are five values between 40 and 49, inclusive, so the percentage of data for that sector is $\frac{5}{16} \times 100\% \approx 31\%$; $\frac{3}{16} \times 100\% \approx 19\%$ of the data is within the range of 50–59, and $\frac{5}{16} \times 100\% \approx 31\%$ is within the range of 60–69. The pie chart does not show the correct percentage of data in each category.

To draw a cumulative frequency histogram, find the cumulative frequency of the data.

Range	Frequency	Cumulative Frequency
30-39	3	3
40-49	5	8
50-59	3	11
60-69	5	16

The histogram does not show the correct cumulative frequency.

The data points in the line graph in choice D do not correspond to the data points given for the question.

37. D: First find $f(g(x))$ by substituting $x + \frac{3}{2}$ anywhere there is an x in the function $f(x)$ and simplify.

$$\begin{aligned} f(g(x)) &= f\left(x + \frac{3}{2}\right) = 2\left(x + \frac{3}{2}\right) - 3 \\ &= 2x + 2 \times \frac{3}{2} - 3 \\ &= 2x + 3 - 3 \\ &= 2x \end{aligned}$$

So the statement that $f(g(z)) = 6$ is equivalent to $2z = 6$. Dividing both sides of this equation by 2, we find $z = 3$.

38. D: Since there are 100 homes' market times represented in each set, the median time a home spends on the market is between the 50th and 51st data point in each set. The 50th and 51st data points for Zip Code 1 are six months and seven months, respectively, so the median time a house in Zip Code 1 spends on the market is between six and seven months (6.5 months), which by the realtor's definition of market time is a seven-month market time. The 50th and 51st data points for Zip Code 2 are both thirteen months, so the median time a house in Zip Code 2 spends on the market is thirteen months. Therefore, there is a six-month difference between the median of Zip Code 1 and the median of Zip Code 2.

To find the mean market time for 100 houses, find the sum of the market times and divide by 100. If the frequency of a one-month market time is 9, the number 1 is added nine times (1×9), if the frequency of a two-month market time is 10, the number 2 is added ten times (2×10), and so on. So, to find the average market time, divide by 100 the sum of the products of each market time and its corresponding frequency. For Zip Code 1, the mean market time is 7.38 months, which, by the realtor's definition of market time, is an eight-month market time. For Zip Code 2, the mean market time is 12.74, which, by the realtor's definition of market time, is a thirteen-month market time. Therefore, the difference between the mean of Zip Code 1 and the mean of Zip Code 2 is 5 months.

The mode market time is the market time for which the frequency is the highest. For Zip Code 1, the mode market time is three months, and for Zip Code 2, the mode market time is eleven months. Therefore, the median time a house spends on the market in Zip Code 1 is less than the mean time a house spends on the market in Zip Code 1.

39. B: This problem can be solved using proportions. Determine the number of feet between the two points by setting up the following proportion.

$$\frac{1 \text{ in}}{10 \text{ ft}} = \frac{24 \text{ in}}{x \text{ ft}}$$

Cross multiply to solve for x.

$$1 \times x = 24 \times 10$$
$$x = 240$$

Therefore, the two points are 240 feet apart. From here, convert 240 feet to a distance in yards. To do so, multiply by the conversion factor $\frac{1\text{ yd}}{3\text{ ft}}$.

$$240\text{ ft} \times \frac{1\text{ yd}}{3\text{ ft}} = 80\text{ yd}$$

The two points are 80 yards apart.

40. C: To find the volume of square pyramid use the formula $A = \frac{1}{3}lwh$, where l is the length of the base, w is the width of the base, and h is the height of the pyramid. The volume of the greenhouse is $\frac{x^2y}{3}$. If the height were increased by 4 ft, the volume would be $\frac{x^2(y+4)}{3} = \frac{x^2y+4x^2}{3}$. Notice this is the volume of the greenhouse, $\frac{x^2y}{3}$, increased by $\frac{4x^2}{3}$.

41. C: First, calculate how much he had at the end of the first week by subtracting \$45 from the amount he invested.

$$\$150 - \$45 = \$105$$

Since he tripled his money the second week, multiply this value by 3.

$$\$105 \times 3 = \$315$$

The man has \$315 at the end of the second week.

42. C: First, multiply the numerator and denominator by the denominator's conjugate, $3 - 2i$. Then, simplify the result and write the answer in the form $a + bi$.

$$\begin{aligned}\frac{2-5i}{3+2i} \times \frac{3-2i}{3-2i} &= \frac{6-4i-15i+10i^2}{9-4i^2}\\ &= \frac{6-19i-10}{9+4}\\ &= \frac{-4-19i}{13}\\ &= -\frac{4}{13} - \frac{19}{13}i\end{aligned}$$

43. D: ΔABC is similar to the smaller triangle with which it shares vertex B.

$$AB = (2x+1) + (x+2) = 3x + 3$$
$$BC = 4 + 6 = 10$$

Set up a proportion and solve for x.

$$\frac{3x+3}{10} = \frac{x+2}{4}$$
$$4(3x+3) = 10(x+2)$$
$$12x + 12 = 10x + 20$$
$$2x = 8$$
$$x = 4$$

So, $AB = 3x + 3 = 3(4) + 3 = 15$.

44. B: Complex numbers are multiplied out in the same manner as algebraic factors.

$$(6+5i)(3-3i) = 18 - 18i + 15i - 15i^2$$

Since $i = \sqrt{-1}$, substitute -1 for i^2.

$$18 - 3i - 15(-1) = 18 + 15 - 3i = 33 - 3i$$

Therefore, the product of the complex numbers $6 + 5i$ and $3 - 3i$ is $33 - 3i$.

45. D: Evaluating $\frac{|x-4|}{2-x}$ when $x = 2$ produces a fraction with a zero denominator. To find the limit as x approaches 2 from the left, sketch a graph or make a table of values.

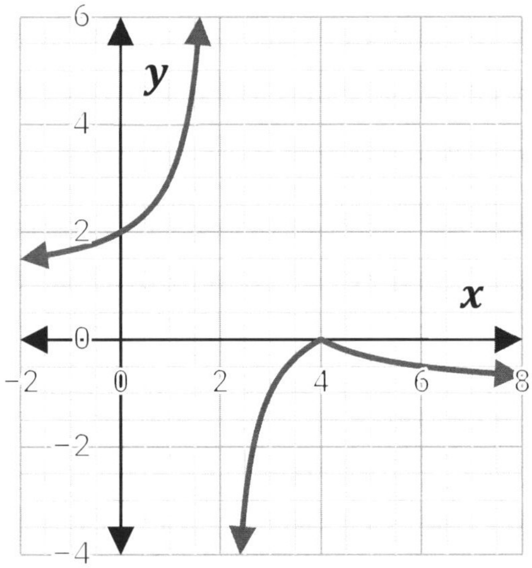

The value of the function approaches ∞ as x approaches 2 from the left, so $\lim_{x\to 2^-} \frac{|x-4|}{2-x} = \infty$.

46. D: A system of linear equations can be solved by using matrices or by using the graphing, substitution, or elimination method. The elimination method is shown here.

$$\begin{cases} -4x + 3y = 8 \\ 6x - 2y = -7 \end{cases}$$

To eliminate y by the elimination method, multiply the top equation by 2 and the bottom equation by 3 so that the coefficients of the y-terms will be additive inverses.

$$2(-4x + 3y) = (8)2 \qquad 3(6x - 2y) = (-7)(3)$$
$$-8x + 6y = 16 \qquad 18x - 6y = -21$$

Then, add the two equations and solve for x.

$$\begin{array}{rrrl} & -8x & +6y & = \ \ 16 \\ + & 18x & -6y & = -21 \\ \hline & & 10x & = \ -5 \\ & & x & = -\frac{1}{2} \end{array}$$

Substitute $-\frac{1}{2}$ for x in either of the given equations and solve for y.

$$\begin{aligned} -4x + 3y &= 8 \\ -4\left(-\frac{1}{2}\right) + 3y &= 8 \\ 2 + 3y &= 8 \\ 3y &= 6 \\ y &= 2 \end{aligned}$$

The solution to the system of equations is $\left(-\frac{1}{2}, 2\right)$.

47. D: For the Final, the third quartile is 87. Since 75% of the data in a set is below the third quartile, there is a 75% chance, or a probability of 0.75, that a test score chosen at random from the Final scored below 87.

48. B: First, apply the laws of exponents to simplify the expression on the left. Then, find a common denominator to add the fractions.

$\frac{(x^2y)(2xy^{-2})^3}{16x^5y^2} + \frac{3}{xy}$	
$\frac{(x^2y)(8x^3y^{-6})}{16x^5y^2} + \frac{3}{xy}$	Simplify the second term in the left numerator using the exponent rule $(x^m)^n = x^{m \cdot n}$.
$\frac{8x^5y^{-5}}{16x^5y^2} + \frac{3}{xy}$	Simplify the numerator of the left fraction using the exponent rule $x^m \cdot x^n = x^{m+n}$.
$\frac{1}{2y^7} + \frac{3}{xy}$	Simplify the left fraction using the exponent rule $\frac{x^m}{x^n} = x^{m-n}$.
$\frac{1}{2y^7} \cdot \frac{x}{x} + \frac{3}{xy} \cdot \frac{2y^6}{2y^6}$	Create common denominators between the two fractions.
$\frac{x}{2xy^7} + \frac{6y^6}{2xy^7}$	Simplify the multiplication.
$\frac{x + 6y^6}{2xy^7}$	Add the two numerators over the common denominator.

49. A: First, write three equations from the information given in the problem. Since the total number of tickets sold was 810, $x + y + z = 810$. The ticket sales generated $14,500, so $15x + 25y + 20z = 14{,}500$. The number of children under ten was the same as twice the number of adults and seniors, so $x = 2(y + z)$, which can be rewritten as $x - 2y - 2z = 0$.

The coefficients of each equation are arranged in the rows of a 3×3 matrix, which, when multiplied by the 3×1 matrix arranging the variables x, y, and z, will give the 3×1 matrix which arranges the constants of the equations.

50. C: The movement of the weight can be described by graphing height h in inches as a function of time t in seconds. Notice that the height is 4.5 in above the table at time 0 since the weight was pulled down 1.5 inches from its starting position 6 inches above the table. The spring fluctuates 1.5 inches above and below its equilibrium point, so its maximum height is 7.5 inches above the table. The graph represents a cosine curve that has been inverted, stretched vertically by a factor of 1.5, and shifted up 6 units; also, the graph has been compressed horizontally, with a period of 0.5 rather than 2π. So, the height of the weight on the spring as a function of time is $h = -1.5\cos(4\pi t) + 6$.

51. B: The line through the center of the box represents the median. The median test score for English and History is the same, not the mean test score, which makes choice B the correct answer. Note that for Science, the median is a better representation of the data than the mean. There is at least one outlier (a point that lies outside of two standard deviations from the mean), which brings down the average test score. In cases such as this, the mean is not the best measure of central tendency, so choice A is not the correct answer. The median of the History scores is 87, and the 3rd quartile scores for Math is also 87, so choice C is not the answer. The median of the English scores is 86, and based on the spread of data, the mean is lower than the median, so choice D is also not correct.

52. C: The center of the sphere is shared by the center of the cube, and each of the corners of the cube touches the surface of the sphere. Therefore, the diameter of the sphere is the line that passes through the center of the cube and connects one corner of the cube to the opposite corner. In the illustration below, notice that the diameter d of the sphere can be represented as the hypotenuse of a right triangle with a short leg measuring 4 units. (Since the volume of the cube is 64 cubic units, each of its sides measures $\sqrt[3]{64} = 4$ units.) The long leg of the triangle is the diagonal of the base of the cube.

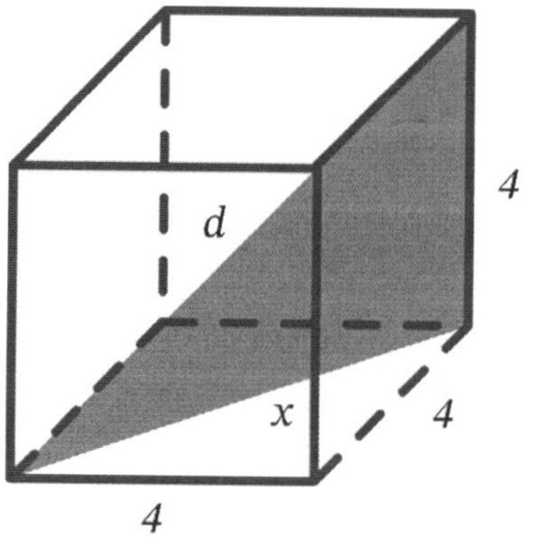

The length of the long leg can be found using the Pythagorean theorem:

$$x^2 = 4^2 + 4^2 = 32$$
$$x = \sqrt{32} = 4\sqrt{2}$$

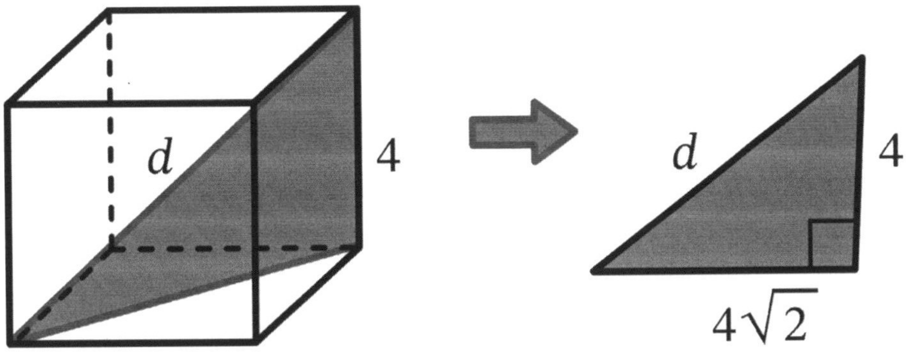

Use the Pythagorean theorem again to find d, the diameter of the sphere:

$$d^2 = \left(4\sqrt{2}\right)^2 + 4^2 = 32 + 16 = 48$$
$$d = \sqrt{48} = 4\sqrt{3}$$

To find the volume of the sphere, use the formula $V = \frac{4}{3}\pi r^3$. Since the radius r of the sphere is half the diameter, $r = 2\sqrt{3}$, and $V = \frac{4}{3}\pi(2\sqrt{3})^3 = \frac{4}{3}\pi\left(24\sqrt{3}\right) = 32\pi\sqrt{3}$ cubic units.

53. C: To evaluate a limit going to infinity, look at the degree of the numerator (call it N) and the degree of the denominator (call it D). If $N > D$, the limit is $\pm\infty$. If $N < D$, the limit is 0. If $N = D$, the limit equals the coefficient of the highest exponent's term in the numerator divided by the coefficient of the highest exponent's term in the denominator. Since $N = D = 2$ for this function, divide the coefficient of the x^2 term in the numerator (1) by the coefficient of the x^2 term in the denominator (2) to find the limit: $\frac{1}{2}$.

54. D: 131 of 283 eleventh graders are male. It is given that an eleventh grader is chosen to attend the conference, so the probability that a male is chosen is $\frac{\text{number of 11th grade males}}{\text{number of 11th graders}} = \frac{131}{283} \approx 0.46$.

55. D: To determine the number of questions Joshua must answer correctly, consider the number of points he must earn. Joshua will receive 4 points for each question he answers correctly, and x represents the number of questions. Therefore, Joshua will receive a total of $4x$ points for all the questions he answers correctly. Joshua must earn more than 92 points. Therefore, to determine the number of questions he must answer correctly, solve the inequality $4x > 92$.

56. B: The difference of two vectors is equal to the difference of their components.

$$v - w = \left((0 - 2), (5 - 1)\right) = (-2,4)$$

To multiply a vector by a scalar, multiply each component by that scalar.

$$3(-2, 4) = (-2 \times 3, 4 \times 3) = (-6, 12)$$

57. B: The recursive definition of the sequence gives the first term of the series, $a_1 = 2$. The definition also defines each term in the series as the sum of the previous term and -3. Therefore, the second term in the series is $2 + (-3) = -1$, the third term in the series is $-1 + (-3) = -4$, and so on.

n	a_n
1	2
2	-1
3	-4

The relationship between n and a_n is linear, so the equation of the sequence can be found using the explicit formula for an arithmetic sequence, $a_n = a_1 + d(n-1)$, where a_n is the value of any term n, a_1 is the value of the first term, and d is the common difference between each term. The value of a_n decreases by 3 each time the value of n increases by 1, so the common difference (d) is -3.

Substitute all the known values into the equation for the explicit formula for an arithmetic sequence, and simplify the formula.

$$a_n = 2 + (-3)(n-1)$$
$$a_n = 2 - 3n + 3$$
$$a_n = -3n + 5$$

58. C: We count the number of sixes that were rolled and divide by the number of total rolls to find the probability.

$$\frac{8 \times 1 + 7 \times 2}{25 \times 2} = \frac{22}{50} = \frac{11}{25} = 0.44$$

59. A: First, subtract the matrices in parentheses, then multiply the resulting matrices together.

$$\begin{aligned}[2 \quad 0 \quad -5]\begin{bmatrix}(4-3)\\(2-5)\\(-1-(-5))\end{bmatrix} &= [2 \quad 0 \quad -5]\begin{bmatrix}1\\-3\\4\end{bmatrix}\\ &= [(2)(1) + (0)(-3) + (-5)(4)]\\ &= [-18]\end{aligned}$$

Note that the product of a 1×3 matrix and a 3×1 matrix, in that order, is a 1×1 matrix. If the order was reversed, the product would be a 3×3 matrix.

60. C: When a figure is reflected twice over non-parallel lines, the resulting transformation is a rotation about the point of intersection of the two lines of reflection. The two lines of reflection $y = x - 3$ and $x = 0$ intersect at $(0, -3)$. So, $\Delta A''B''C''$ represents a rotation of ΔABC about the point $(0, -3)$. The angle of rotation is equal to twice the angle between the two lines of reflection when measured in a counterclockwise direction from the first to the second line of reflection. Since the angle between the lines or reflection measures 45°, the angle of rotation equivalent to the composition of the two reflections measures 90°.

61. D: Rafael's profit on each computer is given by the difference between the price he pays and the price he charges his customer, or \$800 − \$450. If he sells n computers in a month, his total profit will be n times this difference, or $n(\$800 - \$450)$. However, it is necessary to subtract his fixed costs of $3,000 from this to compute his final profit per month. This gives the complete equation:

$$P = n(\$800 - \$450) - \$3{,}000$$

62. B: The inequality is solved by writing a double inequality equivalent to the given inequality but without the absolute value bars.

$$-9 < x + 6 < 9$$

Solve the double inequality by subtracting 6 from all three parts.

$$-15 < x < 3$$

The solution set can be written using interval notation.

$$(-15,3)$$

63. C: A system of linear equations can be solved by using matrices or by using the graphing, substitution, or elimination (also called linear combination) method. The elimination method is shown here:

$$\begin{aligned} 3x + 4y &= 2 \\ 2x + 6y &= -2 \end{aligned}$$

In order to eliminate x by linear combination, multiply the top equation by 2 and the bottom equation by –3 so that the coefficients of the x-terms will be additive inverses.

$$\begin{aligned} 2(3x + 4y &= 2) \\ -3(2x + 6y &= -2) \end{aligned}$$

Then, add the two equations and solve for y.

$$\begin{aligned} 6x + 8y &= 4 \\ \underline{-6x - 18y} &\underline{= 6} \\ -10y &= 10 \\ y &= -1 \end{aligned}$$

Substitute –1 for y in either of the given equations and solve for x.

$$\begin{aligned} 3x + 4y &= 2 \\ 3x + 4(-1) &= 2 \\ 3x - 4 &= 2 \\ 3x &= 6 \\ x &= 2 \end{aligned}$$

The solution to the system of equations is $(2, -1)$.

64. D: To simplify, get as many terms as possible out from the radical as possible. Then, rationalize the denominator to remove any radicals from the denominator.

$$\sqrt{\frac{-54x^5}{80y^6}} = \sqrt{\frac{-9x^4 \times (6x)}{16y^6 \times (5)}}$$
$$= \sqrt{\frac{-(3x^2)^2 \times (6x)}{(4y^3)^2 \times (5)}}$$
$$= \frac{3x^2 i\sqrt{6x}}{4y^3\sqrt{5}} \times \frac{\sqrt{5}}{\sqrt{5}}$$
$$= \frac{3x^2 i\sqrt{30x}}{20y^3}$$

65. A: A coterminal angle for $-\frac{\pi}{4}$ is $2\pi - \frac{\pi}{4} = \frac{7\pi}{4}$.

$$\tan\left(-\frac{\pi}{4}\right) = \tan\left(\frac{7\pi}{4}\right) = \frac{\sin\left(\frac{7\pi}{4}\right)}{\cos\left(\frac{7\pi}{4}\right)}$$

From the unit circle, the values of $\sin\left(\frac{7\pi}{4}\right)$ and $\cos\left(\frac{7\pi}{4}\right)$ are $-\frac{\sqrt{2}}{2}$ and $\frac{\sqrt{2}}{2}$, respectively. Therefore:

$$\tan\left(-\frac{\pi}{4}\right) = \frac{-\frac{\sqrt{2}}{2}}{\frac{\sqrt{2}}{2}} = -1$$

66. D: The area of a triangle is $A = \frac{1}{2}bh$, where b and h are the lengths of the triangle's base and height, respectively. The height of the given triangle is x, but the base is not given. Since the triangle is a right triangle and the hypotenuse is given, the triangle's base can be found using the Pythagorean theorem.

$$x^2 + b^2 = 8^2$$
$$b = \sqrt{64 - x^2}$$

To find the area of the triangle in terms of x, substitute $\sqrt{64 - x^2}$ for the base and x for the height of the triangle into the area formula, $A = \frac{1}{2}bh$.

$$A(x) = \frac{1}{2}(\sqrt{64 - x^2})(x)$$
$$A(x) = \frac{x\sqrt{64 - x^2}}{2}$$

67. B: Determine the probability of each choice.

For choice A, this is the total number of students in the broccoli circle of the Venn diagram divided by the total number of students surveyed:

$$\frac{10+4+3+15}{90}=\frac{32}{90}\approx 35.6\%$$

For choice B, this is the total number of students in the carrots circle and also in at least one other circle divided by the total number in the carrots circle:

$$\frac{15+3+6}{15+3+6+27}=\frac{24}{51}\approx 47.1\%$$

For choice C, this is the number of students in the intersection of all three circles divided by the total number in the overlap of the broccoli and cauliflower circles:

$$\frac{3}{3+4}=\frac{3}{7}\approx 42.9\%$$

For choice D, this is the number of students outside of all the circles divided by the total number of students surveyed:

$$\frac{23}{90}\approx 25.6\%$$

Since choice B has the highest percentage, it is the choice that is most probable.

68. B: First, simplify the expression within the absolute value symbol. Recall, $i^2=-1$.

$$\begin{aligned}(2-3i)^2-(1-4i)&=4-12i+9i^2-1+4i\\&=4-12i-9-1+4i\\&=-6-8i\end{aligned}$$

Therefore, the simplified expression is $-6-8i$.

69. C: The range is the spread of the data. It can be calculated for each subject by subtracting the lowest test score from the highest, or it can be determined visually from the graph. The difference between the highest and lowest test scores in History is $98-72=26$ points. The range for each of the other subjects is greater.

70. C: Choice C is an absolute value function. A function is a relationship in which for every element of the domain (x), there is exactly one element of the range (y). Graphically, a relationship between x and y can be identified as a function if the graph passes the vertical line test.

The first relation is a quartic parabola on its side, which fails the vertical line test for functions. Choice B also fails the vertical line test and is therefore not a function. The relation in choice D pairs two elements of the range with one of the elements of the domain, so it is also not a function.

71. B: The equation of the circle is given in general form. When the equation is written in the standard form $(x-h)^2+(y-k)^2=r^2$, where (h,k) is the center of the circle and r is the radius of the circle, the radius is easy to determine. Putting the equation into standard form requires completing the square for x and y.

$$x^2 + y^2 - 4x + 6y = 5$$
$$(x^2 - 4x + 4) + (y^2 + 6y + 9) = 5 + 4 + 9$$
$$(x - 2)^2 + (y + 3)^2 = 18$$

Since $r^2 = 18$, and since r must be a positive number, $r = \sqrt{18} = 3\sqrt{2}$.

72. D: The graph of $f(x)$ is stretched vertically by a factor of 2 and is inverted with respect to $y = \sin x$, so $a_1 = -2$. The graph of $g(x)$ is stretched vertically by a factor of 4 with respect to the graph of $y = \cos x$, so $a_2 = 4$. Therefore, the statement $a_1 < 0 < a_2$ is true.

73. B: Notice that $x = 1$ results in a zero in the denominator, so choice C cannot be correct since $x \neq 1$. To solve, subtract $\frac{2}{x-1}$ from both sides, then cross-multiply.

$\frac{x-2}{x-1} = \frac{x-1}{x+1} + \frac{2}{x-1}$	Write out the original equation.
$\frac{x-4}{x-1} = \frac{x-1}{x+1}$	Subtract $\frac{2}{x-1}$ from both sides.
$(x+1)(x-4) = (x-1)(x-1)$	Cross multiply.
$x^2 - 3x - 4 = x^2 - 2x + 1$	Multiply the binomials on both sides.
$-3x - 4 = -2x + 1$	Subtract x^2 from both sides.
$-4 = x + 1$	Add $3x$ to both sides.
$-5 = x$	Subtract 1 from both sides.

74. C: There are three ways in which two women from the same department can be selected: two women can be selected from Biology, two women can be selected from Chemistry, or two women can be selected from Physics. Since the events of choosing one woman and then another are both independent events, multiply the two probabilities together to get the probability of choosing two women from the same department.

Biology	**Chemistry**	**Physics**
$\frac{26}{129} \times \frac{25}{128} = \frac{650}{16{,}512}$	$\frac{31}{129} \times \frac{30}{128} = \frac{930}{16{,}512}$	$\frac{20}{129} \times \frac{19}{128} = \frac{380}{16{,}512}$

Since any of these is a distinct possible outcome, the probability that two women will be selected from the same department is the sum of these outcomes.

$$\frac{650}{16{,}512} + \frac{930}{16{,}512} + \frac{380}{16{,}512} = \frac{1{,}960}{16{,}512} \approx 0.119 = 11.9\%$$

75. A: The slope of the line tangent to the graph of a function f at $x = a$ is $f'(a)$. First, find the derivative of $f(x)$.

$$f(x) = -2x^2 - 7$$
$$f'(x) = 2(-2)x^{(2-1)} - 0$$
$$f'(x) = -4x$$

So, to find the slope at $x = 1$, substitute 1 into this derivative.

$$f'(1) = (-4)(1) = -4$$

Therefore, the slope of the line tangent to the graph of $f(x)$ at $x = 1$ is -4.

76. D: To solve the equation, write $x^4 + 9 = 10x^2$ in quadratic form:

$$x^4 - 10x^2 + 9 = 0$$

This trinomial can be factored as $(x^2 - 1)(x^2 - 9) = 0$. Each set of parentheses contains a difference of squares, which can be factored further as $(x + 1)(x - 1)(x + 3)(x - 3) = 0$. Use the zero-product property to find the solutions to the equation.

$x + 1 = 0$	$x - 1 = 0$	$x + 3 = 0$	$x - 3 = 0$
$x = -1$	$x = 1$	$x = -3$	$x = 3$

Therefore, the solutions to this equation are $x = \{-3, -1, 1, 3\}$.

77. D: The first function shifts the graph of $y = \frac{1}{x}$ to the right one unit and down two units. The domain and range of $y = \frac{1}{x}$ are $\{x: x \neq 0\}$ and $\{y: y \neq 0\}$, so the domain and range of $y = \frac{1}{x-1} - 2$ are $\{x: x \neq 1\}$ and $\{y: y \neq -2\}$. The element -2 is not in its range.

The second function shifts the graph of $y = \sqrt{x}$ to the right one unit and up four units. The domain and range of $y = \sqrt{x}$ are $\{x: x \geq 0\}$ and $\{y: y \geq 0\}$, so the domain and range of $y = \frac{\sqrt{x-1}}{4} + 4$ are $\{x: x \geq 1\}$ and $\{y: y \geq 4\}$. The domain does not contain the element -1, and the range does not contain the element -2.

The third function shifts the graph of $y = |x|$ to the right one unit and down one unit. The domain of $y = |x|$ is the set of all real numbers and range is $\{y: y \geq 0\}$, so the domain of $y = |x - 1| - 1$ is the set of all real numbers and the range is $\{y: y \geq -1\}$. The range does not contain the element -2.

The domain of the piecewise function is the set of all real numbers. The range can be found by looking at the equations of the two lines in the piecewise function. When $x < -1$, the graph is an increasing line. When $x \geq -1$, the graph is a decreasing line. Therefore, the domain will be any y-value less than the value of the function when $x = -1$. When $x = -1$, $y = -(-1) + 1 = 2$.

Therefore, the domain is $y \leq 2$. The domain contains the element –1 and the range contains the element –2.

78. C: The volume of the paperweight is $\frac{x^2z}{3}$. If each side of the square base were increased by $\frac{1}{2}$ in, the volume would be $\frac{\left(x+\frac{1}{2}\right)^2 z}{3} = \frac{\left(x^2+x+\frac{1}{4}\right)(z)}{3} = \frac{x^2z+xz+\frac{1}{4}z}{3} = \frac{x^2z}{3} + \frac{4xz+z}{12}$. So, the original volume of the paperweight, $\frac{x^2z}{3}$, increased by $\frac{4xz+z}{12}$, or $\frac{z(4x+1)}{12}$.

79. C: If all possible outcomes are equally likely, then the probability of an event is the number of outcomes in which that event occurs, divided by the number of possible outcomes. A camper who is at least eight years old can be eight, nine, or ten years old, so the probability of randomly selecting a camper at least eight years old is:

$$\frac{\text{number of eight-, nine-, and ten-year-old campers}}{\text{total number of campers}} = \frac{14+12+10}{12+15+14+12+10} = \frac{36}{63} = \frac{4}{7}$$

80. C: If the sine of one angle is equal to the cosine of another, this means that the two angles are complementary. Complementary angles add up to 90°. So, $m + n = 90$, and therefore $(3x + 12) + (-x + 32) = 90$. We combine like terms to obtain $2x + 44 = 90$. We subtract 44 from each side to get $2x = 46$. Finally, we divide each side by 2 to find that $x = 23$. Choice A is incorrect because it is obtained by setting m and n equal to each other. Choice B is incorrect because it is the value of n. Choice D is incorrect because it is the value of m.

81. B: Since ΔADC is a right triangle with legs measuring 5 and 12, its hypotenuse measures 13. (5-12-13 is a Pythagorean triple.)

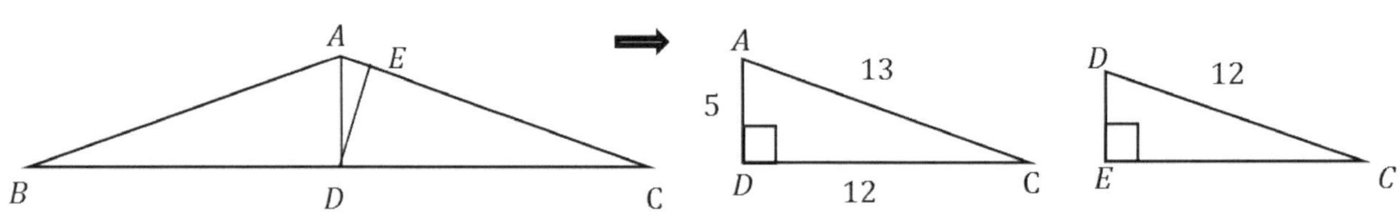

ΔADC and ΔDEC are both right triangles that share vertex C. By the angle-angle similarity theorem, $\Delta ADC \sim \Delta DEC$. Therefore, a proportion can be written and solved to find DE.

$$\frac{5}{DE} = \frac{13}{12}$$
$$13DE = 60$$
$$DE \approx 4.6$$

82. B: To simplify the inequality $2 - \frac{1}{2}x < 1$, we can first subtract 2 from both sides.

$$2 - \frac{1}{2}x - 2 < 1 - 2$$
$$-\frac{1}{2}x < -1$$

Now, we can divide both sides of the inequality by −1. When an inequality is multiplied or divided by a negative number, it flips ($<$ becomes $>$, $\leq$ becomes $\geq$, and vice versa). So $-\frac{1}{2}x < -1$ becomes $\frac{1}{2}x > 1$. We then multiply both sides by 2 to yield $x > 2$.

83. A: Find the points of intersection of the two graphs.

$$x^2 - 2x - 12 = x - 2$$
$$x^2 - 3x - 10 = 0$$
$$(x + 2)(x - 5) = 0$$
$$x = -2, x = 5$$

So, the area is between the graphs on the interval $[-2,5]$. To determine which of the graphs is the upper or lower bound, pick a test point in the interval. Using $x = 0$ as the test point:

$$\begin{array}{ll} y = (0)^2 - 2(0) - 12 & y = (0) - 2 \\ y = -12 & y = -2 \end{array}$$

The finite region is bound at the top by the line $y = x - 2$ and at the bottom by $y = x^2 - 2x - 12$, and the height of the region at point x is defined by $[(x - 2) - (x^2 - 2x - 12)]$, so the area is:

$$\begin{aligned} A &= \int_{-2}^{5} [(x - 2) - (x^2 - 2x - 12)]dx \\ &= \int_{-2}^{5} (-x^2 + 3x + 10)\, dx \\ &= \left[-\frac{1}{3}x^3 + \frac{3}{2}x^2 + 10x\right]_{-2}^{5} \\ &= \left[-\frac{1}{3}(5)^3 + \frac{3}{2}(5)^2 + 10(5)\right] - \left[-\frac{1}{3}(-2)^3 + \frac{3}{2}(-2)^2 + 10(-2)\right] \\ &= \left[-\frac{125}{3} + \frac{75}{2} + 50\right] - \left[\frac{8}{3} + 6 - 20\right] \\ &= \frac{275}{6} - \left(-\frac{34}{3}\right) \\ &= \frac{343}{6} \end{aligned}$$

84. D: To add the two fractions, first rewrite them with the least common denominator, which is in this case y^3. This is already the denominator in $\frac{x}{y^3}$, and we can rewrite $\frac{x^2}{y^2}$ as $\frac{x^2 \times y}{y^2 \times y} = \frac{x^2y}{y^3}$. Thus, $\frac{x^2}{y^2} + \frac{x}{y^3} = \frac{x^2y}{y^3} + \frac{x}{y^3} = \frac{x^2y + x}{y^3}$.

85. B: The height of the ball is a function of time, so the average rate of change can be found by calculating $\frac{h(3)-h(2)}{3-2}$.

$$\begin{aligned}\frac{h(3)-h(2)}{3-2} &= \frac{[-16(3)^2+56(3)+6]-[-16(2)^2+56(2)+6]}{1} \\ &= (-144+168+6)-(-64+112+6) \\ &= -24\end{aligned}$$

Therefore, the average rate of change in the ball's height with respect to time over this interval is -24 ft/s.

86. C: A height of 5'11", or 71 inches, is one standard deviation above the mean. Since approximately 68% of the data is within one standard deviation of the mean, about 32% (100% − 68%) of the data is outside of one standard deviation within the mean. Normally distributed data is symmetric about the mean, which means that about 16% of the data lies below one standard deviation below the mean and about 16% of data lies above one standard deviation above the mean. Therefore, approximately 16% of individuals are 5'11" or taller, while approximately 84% of the population is shorter than 5'11". Multiply to find 84% of 200, $0.84 \times 200 = 168$. So, about 168 people from the selected group are shorter than 5'11".

87. D: If the distance between the two houses is 10 cm on the map, then the actual distance between the houses is 100 m. To find x, use the Pythagorean theorem.

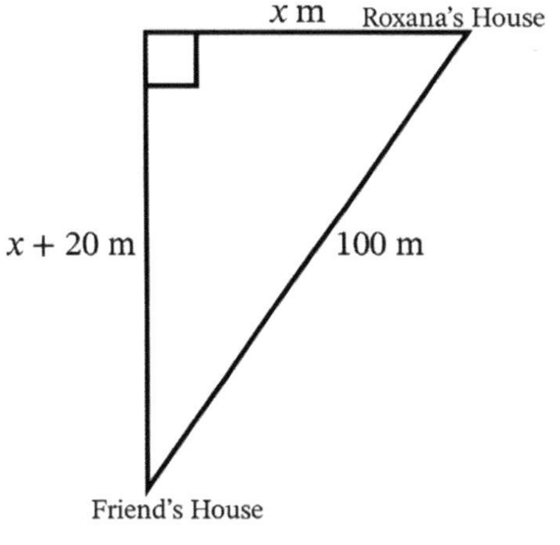

$$\begin{aligned}x^2+(x+20)^2 &= (100)^2 \\ x^2+x^2+40x+400 &= 10{,}000 \\ 2x^2+40x-9{,}600 &= 0 \\ 2(x^2+20x-4{,}800) &= 0 \\ 2(x-60)(x+80) &= 0 \\ x=60 \quad x &= -80\end{aligned}$$

Since x represents a distance, it cannot equal −80. Since $x = 60$, $x + 20 = 80$. Roxana walks a total of $60 + 80 = 140$ meters to get to her friend's house.

88. C: Evaluate the integral by adding 1 to the exponent of each term and dividing the coefficient by the new exponent. Don't forget to add the constant of integration to the end.

$$\int 6x^2 + \frac{1}{2}x - 3\,dx = \frac{6}{2+1}x^{(2+1)} + \frac{\frac{1}{2}}{1+1}x^{(1+1)} - \frac{3}{0+1}x^{(0+1)} + C$$
$$= 2x^3 + \frac{1}{4}x^2 - 3x + C$$

89. D: The longest side of a right triangle, called the hypotenuse, H, can be calculated using the Pythagorean theorem, together with the lengths of the other two sides, which are given as 6 and 8 units.

$$H^2 = (S_1)^2 + (S_2)^2$$
$$H^2 = 6^2 + 8^2$$
$$H^2 = 36 + 64$$
$$H^2 = 100$$
$$\sqrt{H^2} = \sqrt{100}$$
$$H = 10$$

Therefore, using $H = 10$, the perimeter, P, can be calculated as follows: $P = 10 + 6 + 8 = 24$. The perimeter of the triangle is 24 units.

90. A: There are many ways to solve quadratic equations in the form $ax^2 + bx + c = 0$. From the answer choices, the equation must have complex solutions. So, solve this equation by completing the square or by using the quadratic formula, $x = \frac{-b\pm\sqrt{b^2-4ac}}{2a}$. Here we will use the quadratic formula. Given $3x^2 + 6x + 4 = 0$; $a = 3, b = 6, c = 4$:

$$x = \frac{-(6) \pm \sqrt{(6)^2 - 4(3)(4)}}{2(3)}$$
$$x = \frac{-6 \pm \sqrt{36 - 48}}{6}$$
$$x = \frac{-6 \pm \sqrt{-12}}{6}$$
$$x = \frac{-6 \pm 2i\sqrt{3}}{6}$$
$$x = \frac{-3 \pm i\sqrt{3}}{3}$$

Practice Test #2

Refer to the following for question 1:

For a science fair project, Paul wanted to find the probability of rolling an even number with a weighted die versus a fair die. He did fifty tests, rolling the die three times for each test and recording the number of even numbers that came up. The chart below shows his results.

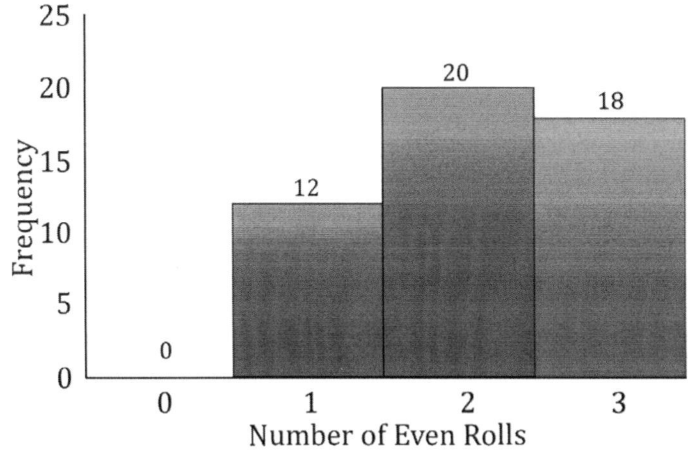

1. Given these experimental data, which of these approximates $P(\text{even})$ for a single roll of this die?

a. 0.468
b. 0.5
c. 0.625
d. 0.707

2. Which of the following correctly represents the solution to the inequality?

$$x^2 + 2x \geq x + 6$$

a. 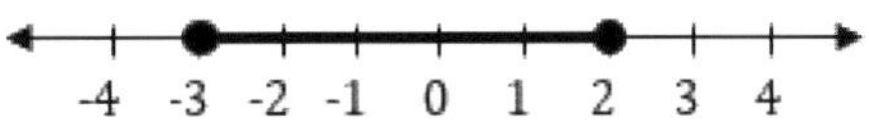

b. 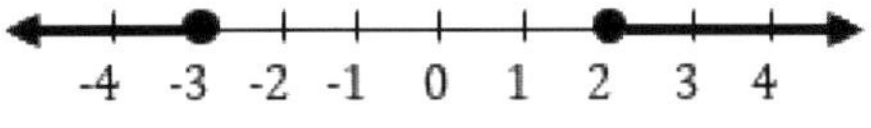

c. 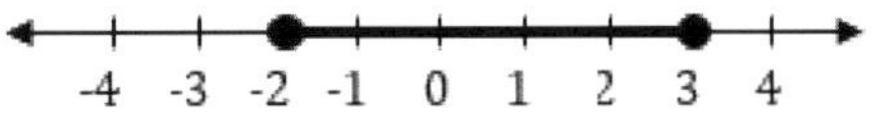

d. 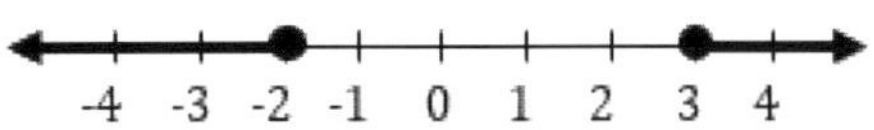

3. If the square of three times the sum of a and six is fourteen more than a, which of these is a possible value of a?

a. $\sqrt{2}$
b. $\frac{3}{2}$
c. 1
d. -5

4. Simplify:

$$\frac{(x^2y^{-3})(4xy)^2}{16x^4y^4} + \frac{3}{2xy}$$

a. $\frac{3x+24y^6}{8xy^7}$
b. $\frac{2x+6y^6}{2xy^4}$
c. $\frac{x+24y^5}{8xy^6}$
d. $\frac{2x+3y^4}{2xy^5}$

5. The ratio of employee wages and benefits to all other operational costs of a business is 2: 3. If a business's total operating expenses are $130,000 per month, how much money does the company spend on employee wages and benefits?

a. $43,333.33
b. $86,666.67
c. $52,000.00
d. $78,000.00

6. Simplify: $\frac{4+i}{3-2i}$

a. $\frac{10}{13} + \frac{11}{13}i$
b. $\frac{21}{13}$
c. $\frac{14}{13} + \frac{11}{13}i$
d. $\frac{10}{13} + \frac{5}{13}i$

7. Find the derivative of: $f(x) = e^{2x^4+2}$

a. e^{8x^3}
b. $(8x^3)e^{2x^4+2}$
c. $(2x^4 + 2)e^{2x^4+2}$
d. $8x^3\ln^{2x^4+2}$

8. What is the exact value of $\tan(-\frac{7\pi}{6})$?

a. $\frac{1}{2}$
b. $-\frac{\sqrt{3}}{3}$
c. $-\frac{\sqrt{3}}{2}$
d. -1

9. Which of these statements is NOT necessarily true when $f(x) = \log_b x$ and $b > 1$?

a. The x-intercept of the graph of $f(x)$ is $(1, 0)$.
b. The graph of $f(x)$ passes through $(b, 1)$.
c. $f(x) < 0$ when $0 < x < 1$.
d. If $g(x) = x^b$, the graph of $f(x)$ is symmetric to the graph of $g(x)$ with respect to $y = x$.

10. Find the sum of the following polynomials.

$$(3x^2 + x + 3) + (8x^2 + 5x + 16)$$

a. $7x^2 + 29\,x^2$
b. $11x^2 + 6x + 19$
c. $30x + 19$
d. $(3x^2 + 3x) + 13x^2 + 16$

11. If $f(x) = \frac{2}{3}x^2 + 4$, find the slope of the line tangent to the graph of $f(x)$ at $x = -3$.

a. -4
b. 0
c. 1
d. $\frac{4}{3}$

Refer to the following for question 12:

This data shows the number of students at a high school who are enrolled in various electives.

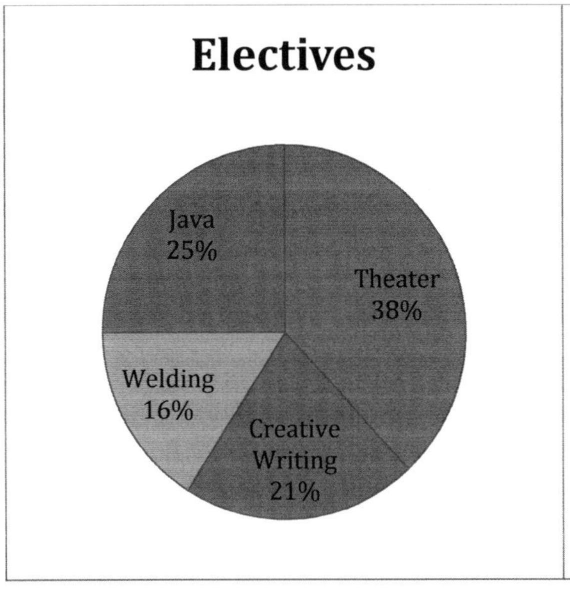

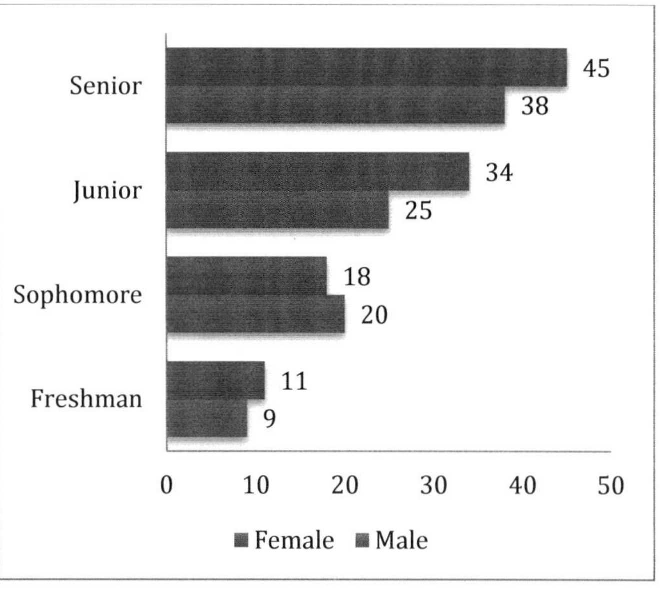

12. Compare the two quantities.

Quantity A	Quantity B
The percentage of students taking Java or Creative Writing	The percentage of students in electives who are male

a. Quantity A is greater.
b. Quantity B is greater.
c. The two quantities are the same.
d. The relationship cannot be determined from the given information.

13. Suppose the path of a baseball hit straight up from 3.5 feet above the ground is modeled by the first quadrant graph of the function $h(t) = -15t^2 + 56t + 3.5$, where t is the flight time of the ball in seconds and h is the height of the ball in feet. What is the velocity of the ball 1.5 seconds after it is hit?

a. 11 ft/s upward
b. 56 ft/s upward
c. 11 ft/s downward
d. 56 ft/s downward

14. A rancher is putting up a rectangular cattle pen. His original plan was too expensive, so he changed to a smaller size, subtracting x feet from each of the original boundaries. By fencing a rectangular space 764 yd^2 smaller than the original plan, the rancher saves $648 in fencing materials, which cost $9 per linear foot. How much does he spend?

a. $5,832
b. $6,552
c. $6,876
d. $7,200

15. Evaluate $\lim_{x \to -3} \frac{x^3+3x^2-x-3}{x^2-9}$.

a. 0
b. $\frac{1}{3}$
c. $-\frac{4}{3}$
d. ∞

16. Simplify: $-2(2 + 6i) - 4(2 - 3i)$.

a. $-12 - 24i$
b. -12
c. $4 - 24i$
d. $4 + 12i$

17. Which of the following is the solution to the inequality $2|x + 3| - 9 \geq -1$.

a. $-1 \leq x \leq 7$
b. $-7 \leq x \leq 1$
c. $x \leq -1$ and $x \geq 7$
d. $x \leq -7$ and $x \geq 1$

18. For vector $v = (-2, -3)$ and vector $w = (0, 4)$, find $\frac{1}{2}(v + w)$.

a. $(-2, 1)$
b. $(-2, -7)$
c. $\left(-1, -\frac{7}{2}\right)$
d. $\left(-1, \frac{1}{2}\right)$

Refer to the following for question 19:

This data shows the number of students at a high school who are enrolled in various electives.

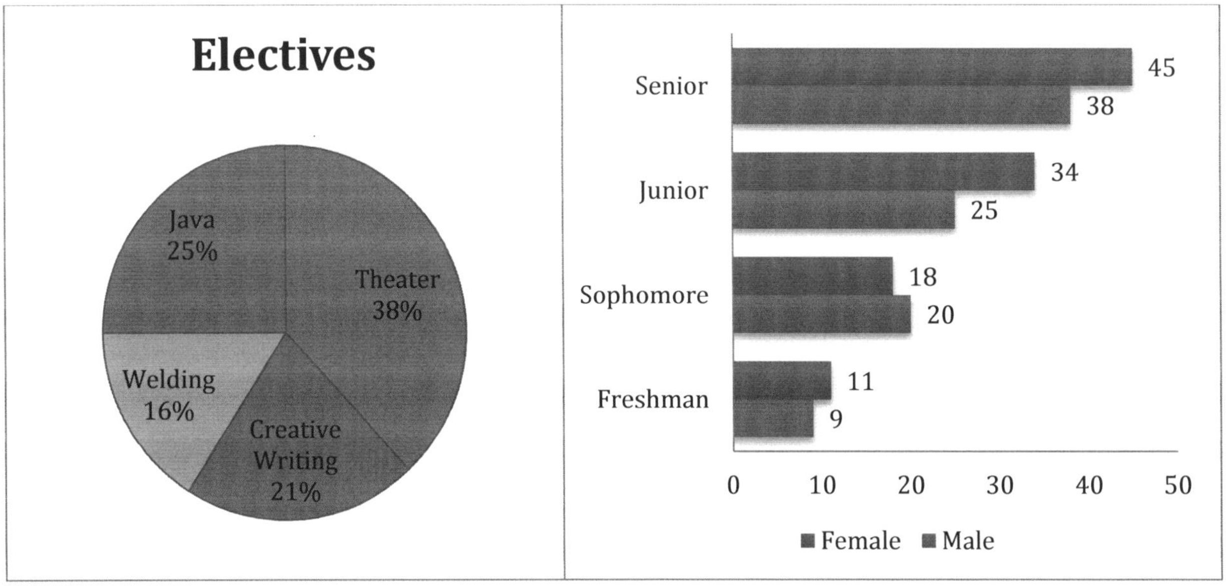

19. A sophomore is randomly selected to be interviewed for the school paper. What is the approximate probability that the student is male?

a. 0.53
b. 0.47
c. 0.19
d. 0.10

20. Simplify:

$$\begin{bmatrix} 1 & -3 & 2 \end{bmatrix} \left(\begin{bmatrix} -3 \\ 2 \\ 1 \end{bmatrix} + \begin{bmatrix} 3 \\ 4 \\ -2 \end{bmatrix} \right)$$

a. $\begin{bmatrix} 0 & -18 & -2 \end{bmatrix}$
b. $\begin{bmatrix} 0 \\ -18 \\ -2 \end{bmatrix}$
c. $\begin{bmatrix} -20 \end{bmatrix}$
d. $\begin{bmatrix} 1 & 0 & 0 \\ -3 & 0 & 6 \\ 2 & 0 & -1 \end{bmatrix}$

21. Milly walks x meters north and $x + 15$ meters east to get to the grocery store. On a neighborhood map which has a scale of 1 cm : 15 m, the distance between Milly's house and the grocery store is 5 cm. How far did Milly walk to the store?

a. 105 m
b. 75 m
c. 60 m
d. 45 m

22. The temperature of a cup of coffee is 98 degrees. If its temperature decreases by 2 degrees per minute, what will its temperature be after 4 minutes?

a. 100 degrees
b. 98 degrees
c. 94 degrees
d. 90 degrees

23. Which of the following expressions gives the area A of the triangle below as a function of sides a and b?

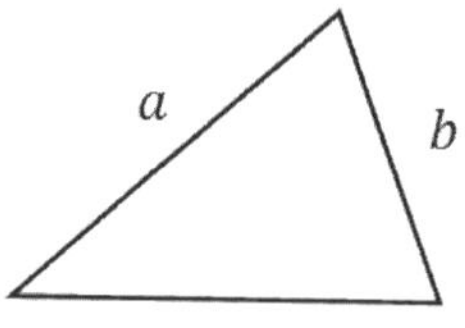

a. $\frac{2a^2-b^2}{4}$
b. $\frac{ab-a^2}{2}$
c. $\frac{b\sqrt{a^2-b^2}}{2}$
d. $\frac{b\sqrt{4a^2-b^2}}{4}$

24. Solve: $\frac{x+2}{x+1} = \frac{x+9}{x+7} + \frac{2}{x+1}$.

a. $x = -3$
b. $x = -1$
c. $x = 1$
d. $x = 5$

25. The velocity of a car that starts at position 0 at time 0 is given by the equation $v(t) = 10t - t^2$ for $0 \leq t \leq 10$. What is the position of the car when its acceleration is 0?

a. 18
b. 25
c. $\frac{175}{6}$
d. $\frac{250}{3}$

26. A circle is inscribed inside quadrilateral $ABCD$. $\overline{CD}$ is bisected by the point at which it is tangent to the circle. If $\overline{AB} = 10$, $\overline{BC} = 12$, and $\overline{CD} = 8$, then what is the length of $\overline{AD}$?

a. $\overline{AD} = 11$
b. $\overline{AD} = 7.5$
c. $\overline{AD} = 6$
d. $\overline{AD} = 2\sqrt{11}$

27. What is the radius of the circle defined by the equation $x^2 + y^2 - 10x + 8y + 29 = 0$?

a. $2\sqrt{3}$
b. $2\sqrt{5}$
c. $\sqrt{29}$
d. 12

28. Vivian has $50. She goes to the store and buys a calculator. Then she buys a book that costs half what the calculator cost. Then she buys a pen that costs half what the book cost. She has $15 left. How much did she spend on the calculator?

a. $14
b. $15
c. $18
d. $20

29. Graph the following piecewise function and use your graph to determine which of the following statements about discontinuities and extrema is correct.

$$f(x) = \begin{cases} 4 - x^2, & \text{if } x < 0 \\ 4 - 2x, & \text{if } 0 \leq x < 2 \\ 7 - x, & \text{if } x \geq 2 \end{cases}$$

a. The function has 2 discontinuities and a maximum value of 7.
b. The function has 1 discontinuity and a maximum of 5.
c. The function has 2 discontinuities and no extrema.
d. The function has no discontinuities and a maximum of 4.

30. If $\sin\theta = \frac{\sqrt{2}}{2}$ when $\frac{\pi}{2} < \theta < \pi$, what is the value of θ?

a. $\frac{\pi}{4}$
b. $\frac{3\pi}{4}$
c. $\frac{2\pi}{3}$
d. $\frac{5\pi}{6}$

31. Which of the following expressions is equal to $\cos\theta\cot\theta$?

a. $\sin\theta$
b. $\sec\theta\tan\theta$
c. $\csc\theta - \sin\theta$
d. $\sec\theta - \sin\theta$

32. Which of these sets forms a group under addition?

a. $\{0\}$
b. $\{1\}$
c. $\{-1,0,1\}$
d. $\{i,-i,1\}$

33. Which of these relationships represent y as a function of x?

a. $x = y^2$

c. $y = |x|$

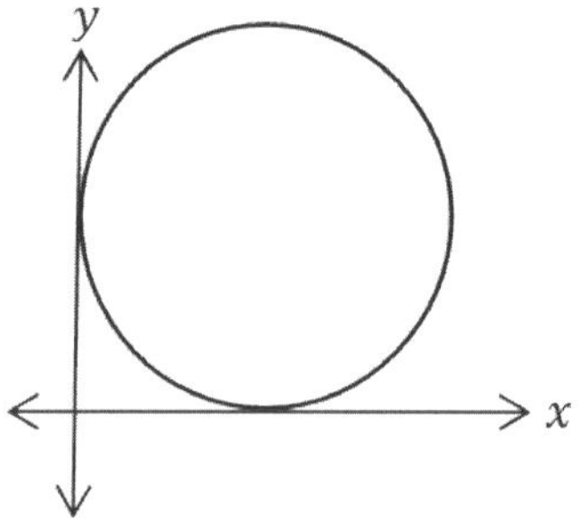

b.

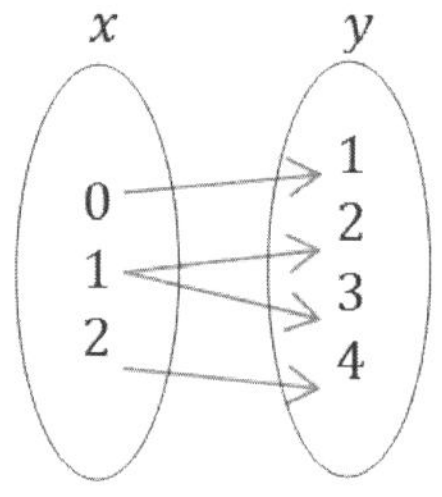

d.

34. A manufacturer wishes to produce a cylindrical can which can hold up to 1 L of liquid. To the nearest tenth, what is the radius of the can that requires the least amount of material to make?

a. 5.4 cm
b. 6.2 cm
c. 9.1 cm
d. 10.8 cm

35. Given the figure and the following information, find DE to the nearest tenth.

$\overline{AD}$ is an altitude of ΔABC
$\overline{DE}$ is an altitude of triangle ΔADC
$\overline{BD} \cong \overline{DC}$
$AB = 17; AD = 8$

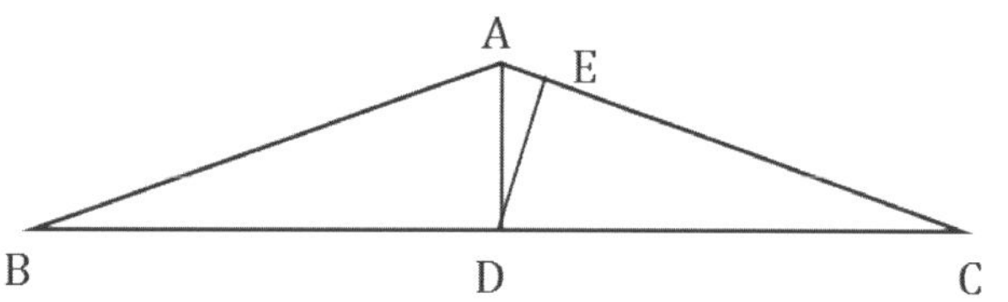

a. 5.8
b. 6.2
c. 6.9
d. 7.1

36. Solve $\sec^2\theta = 2\tan\theta$ for $0 < \theta \leq 2\pi$.

a. $\theta = \frac{\pi}{6}$ or $\frac{7\pi}{6}$
b. $\theta = \frac{\pi}{4}$ or $\frac{5\pi}{4}$
c. $\theta = \frac{3\pi}{4}$ or $\frac{7\pi}{4}$
d. There is no solution to the equation.

Refer to the following for question 37:

The box-and-whisker plot displays student test scores by class period.

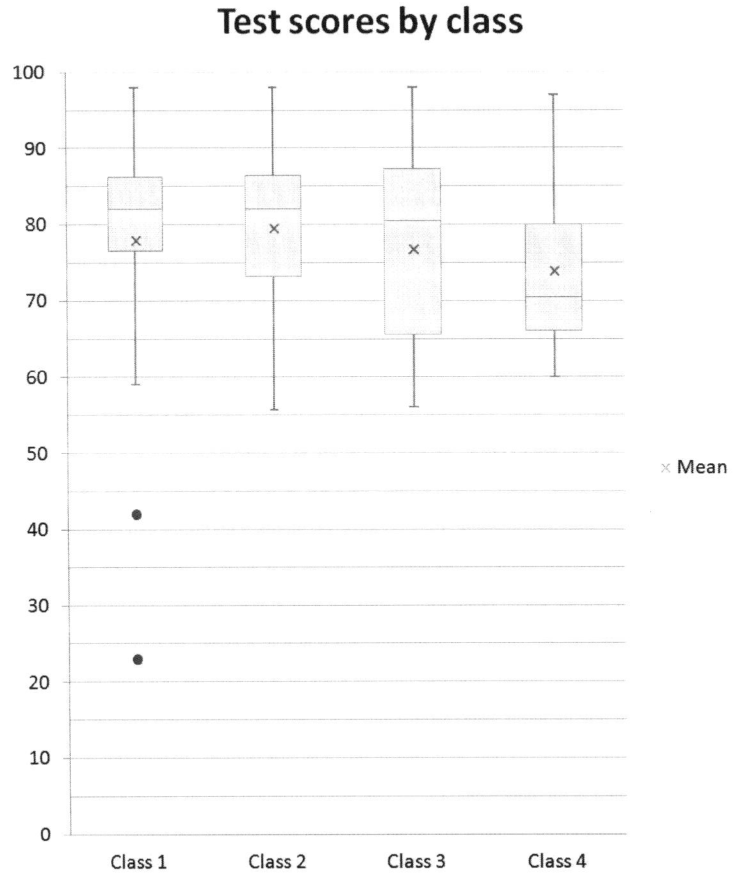

37. What is the probability that a student chosen at random from class 2 made above a 73 on this test?

a. 0.25
b. 0.5
c. 0.6
d. 0.75

38. Given the line $y = -\frac{5}{2}x + 2$, what is the equation of a line parallel to that line that passes through the point $(2, 3)$?

a. $5x + 2y = 16$
b. $-2x + 5y = 11$
c. $-5x + 2y = -4$
d. $2x + 5y = 19$

39. A colony of Escherichia coli is inoculated from a Petri dish into a test tube containing 50 mL of nutrient broth. The test tube is placed in a 37 °C incubator and agitator. After one hour, the number of bacteria in the test tube is determined to be 8×10^6. Given that the doubling time of Escherichia coli is 20 minutes with agitation at 37 °C, approximately how many bacteria should the test tube contain after eight hours of growth?

a. 2.56×10^8
b. 2.05×10^9
c. 1.7×10^{14}
d. 1.7×10^{13}

40. Find $(g \circ f)(x)$ when $f(x) = 3x - 2$ and $g(x) = x^2 - x - 6$.

a. $9x^2 - 6x + 6$
b. $3x^2 - 9x + 8$
c. $9x^2 - 15x$
d. $3x^2 - 12x + 2$

41. For ΔABC, what is the length of $\overline{BC}$?

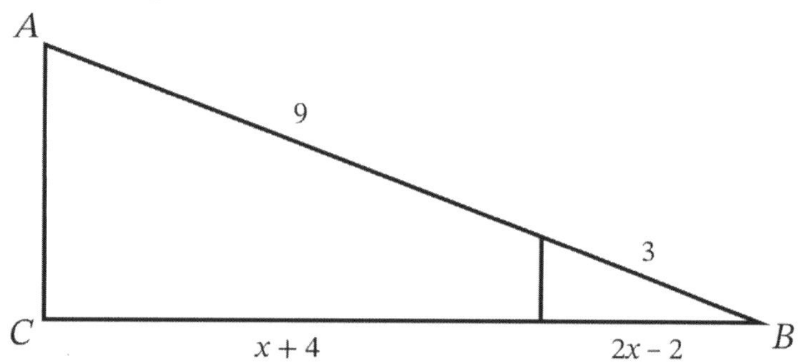

a. 2
b. 6
c. 8
d. 9

42. Which of the following expressions is equivalent to $\frac{2+3i}{4-2i}$?

a. $\frac{1}{10} + \frac{4}{5}i$
b. $\frac{1}{10}$
c. $\frac{7}{6} + \frac{2}{3}i$
d. $\frac{1}{10} + \frac{3}{10}i$

43. Based on ΔABC below, what is the value of x?

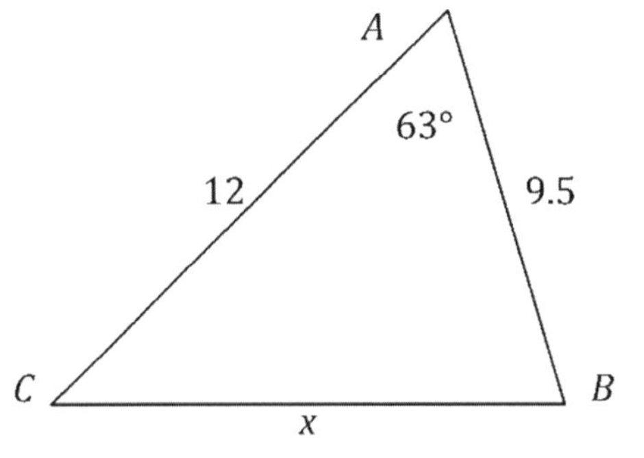

a. 5.6
b. 7.3
c. 11.4
d. 15.3

Refer to the following for question 44:

The box-and-whisker plot displays student test scores assessed throughout a semester to see if students were improving.

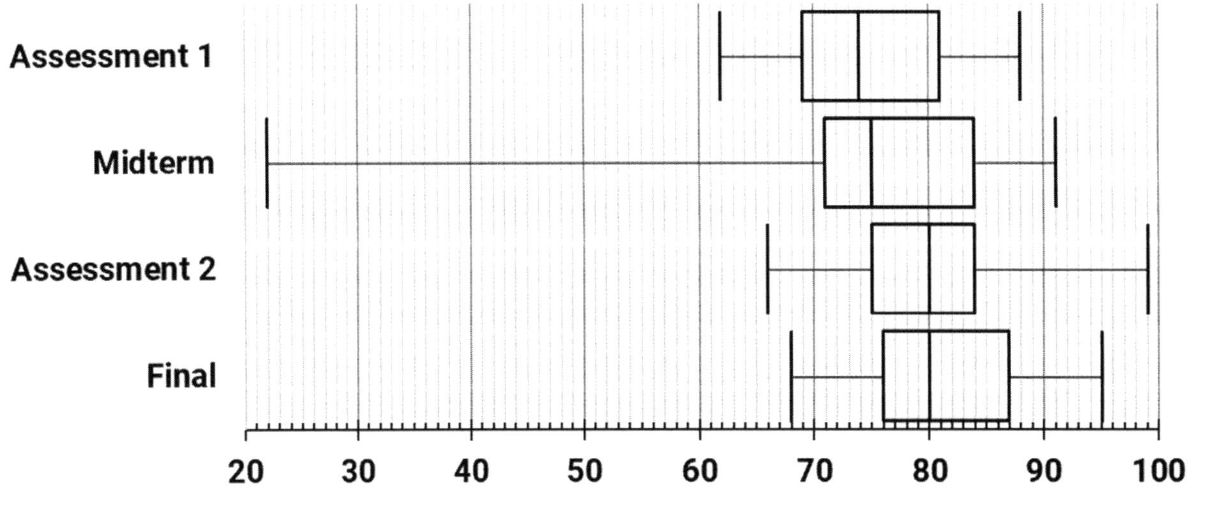

44. Which assessment has the greatest range of test scores?

a. Assessment 1
b. Midterm
c. Assessment 2
d. Final

45. Which of the following represents a function?

a. $\{(2,1), (3,-2), (6,8), (-1,-4), (4,-1)\}$
b. $\{(8,5), (7,9), (3,1), (4,7), (3,6)\}$
c. $\{(-4,6), (2,3), (4,-2), (3,6), (-4,2)\}$
d. $\{(2,6), (6,1), (5,8), (2,-1), (-3,1)\}$

46. Which of these defines the recursive sequence $a_1 = -2, a_{n+1} = a_n + \frac{1}{2}$ explicitly?

a. $a_n = \frac{1}{2}n - 2$
b. $a_n = -2n + \frac{1}{2}$
c. $a_n = \frac{1}{2}n - \frac{5}{2}$
d. $a_n = -2n + \frac{5}{2}$

Refer to the following for question 47:

The diagrams below show the number of people in a small town who participate in various types of volunteer work.

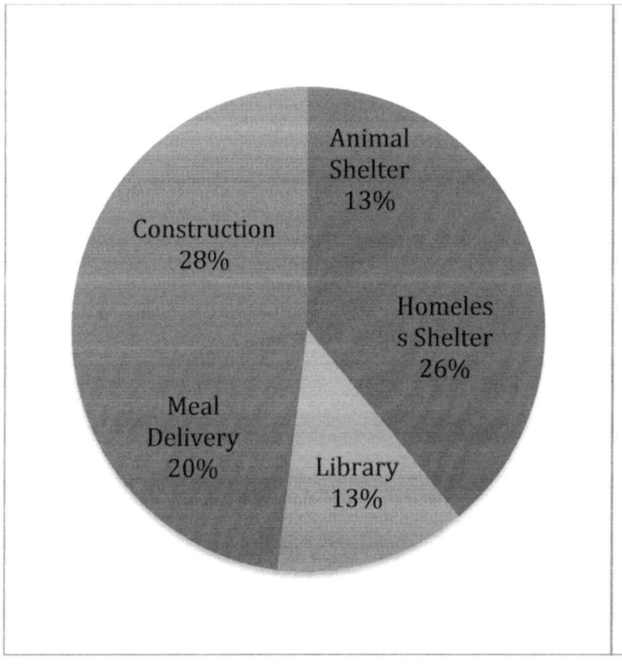

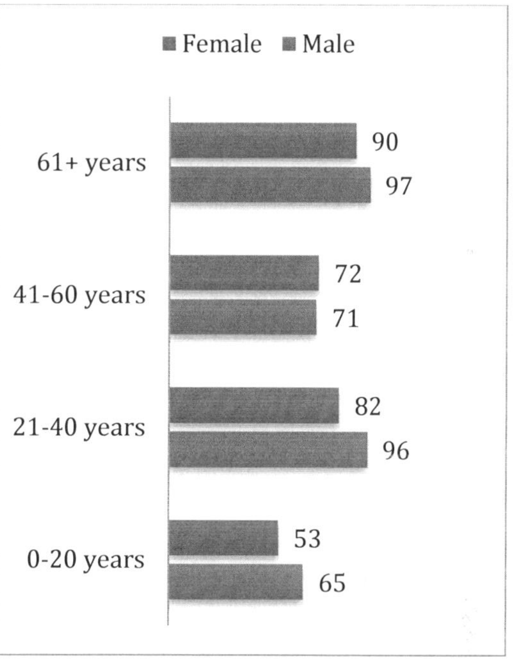

47. A volunteer under age 21 is chosen at random for a scholarship. What is the approximate probability that the student is male?

a. 0.47
b. 0.51
c. 0.55
d. 0.58

48. A student devises a method for constructing the center of a circle and asks you to evaluate it. The method involves drawing two chords of the circle and constructing their perpendicular bisectors. The point at which the perpendicular bisectors intersect is the center of the circle. How do you evaluate this method?

a. You congratulate the student on finding a clever construction that always works.
b. You congratulate the student on finding a clever construction that works in general, but you explain that it fails in a special case.
c. You explain that the method fails in general, though it often produces a point deceptively close to the center, but works in a special case.
d. You explain that the method always fails though it often produces a point deceptively close to the center.

49. Evaluate $\lim_{x\to\infty} \frac{4x^2+2x-1}{2x^2-3}$.

a. 0
b. $\frac{1}{2}$
c. 2
d. ∞

50. A line passes through the points $(-3, 18)$ and $(5, 2)$. What is the slope of the line?

a. -2
b. $-\frac{1}{2}$
c. $\frac{1}{2}$
d. 2

51. Simplify $\sqrt{\frac{-32x^4}{75y^5}}$.

a. $\frac{2x^2 i\sqrt{2y}}{9y^3}$
b. $\frac{4x^2 i\sqrt{6y}}{15y^3}$
c. $\frac{-2x^2\sqrt{21y}}{9y^3}$
d. $\frac{8x^3 i\sqrt{6y}}{27y^2}$

52. A target is made of concentric circles, as shown below. The width of each band is a and the center is a circle with radius a. Which of the following gives the area A of the shaded region as a function of a?

a. $A = 12\pi a^2$
b. $A = 15\pi a^2$
c. $A = 18\pi a^2$
d. $A = 25\pi a^2$

53. A two-digit number is chosen at random. What is the probability that the chosen number is a multiple of 7?

a. $\frac{1}{10}$
b. $\frac{1}{9}$
c. $\frac{11}{90}$
d. $\frac{13}{90}$

54. Which of these is equivalent to $\log_y 64$ if $2\log_8 y + \log_8 4 = 2$?

a. 1
b. 2
c. 3
d. 6

55. A teacher recorded the dates that students turned in projects in two different classes to compare trends and noticed that a large number of students were submitting their work late. She plotted charts to see how many students in each class were turning in late work and how late they were.

Which of the following is a true statement for these data?

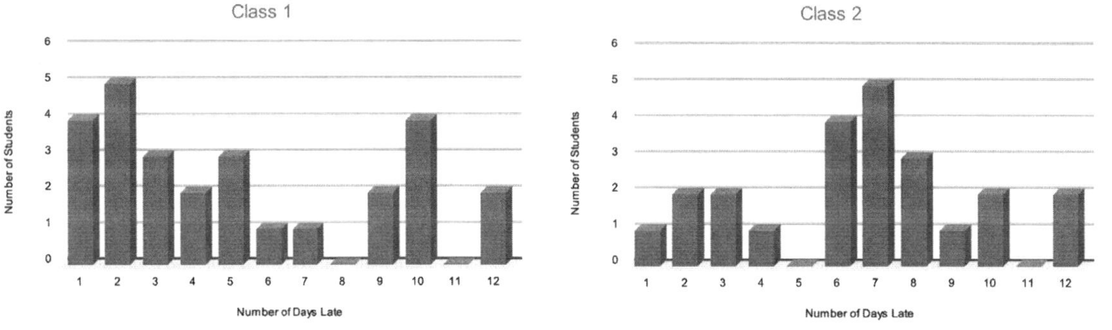

a. The median number of days late in Class 1 is 2 days less than in Class 2.
b. On average, students turned in work 4 days later in Class 2 than in Class 1 (round to nearest whole number).
c. The mode late time is higher for Class 2 than for Class 1.
d. The median late time for Class 1 is greater than the mean for Class 1.

56. A shirt is marked down by 25% and placed on a clearance rack, on which is posted a sign reading, "Take an extra 30% off already reduced merchandise." What fraction of the original price is the final sale price of the shirt?

a. $\frac{9}{20}$
b. $\frac{11}{20}$
c. $\frac{21}{40}$
d. $\frac{7}{10}$

57. Which of these functions includes 2 as an element of the domain and –3 as an element of the range?

a. $y = \frac{1}{x+1} - 3$
b. $y = \sqrt{x-2} - 3$
c. $y = |x-1| + 3$
d. $y = \begin{cases} -2x & x < -1 \\ x + 3 & x \geq -1 \end{cases}$

Refer to the following for question 58:

Below are graphed the functions $f(x) = a_1 \sin(b_1 x)$ and $g(x) = a_2 \cos(b_2 x)$; a_1, a_2, b_1, and b_2 are positive rational numbers.

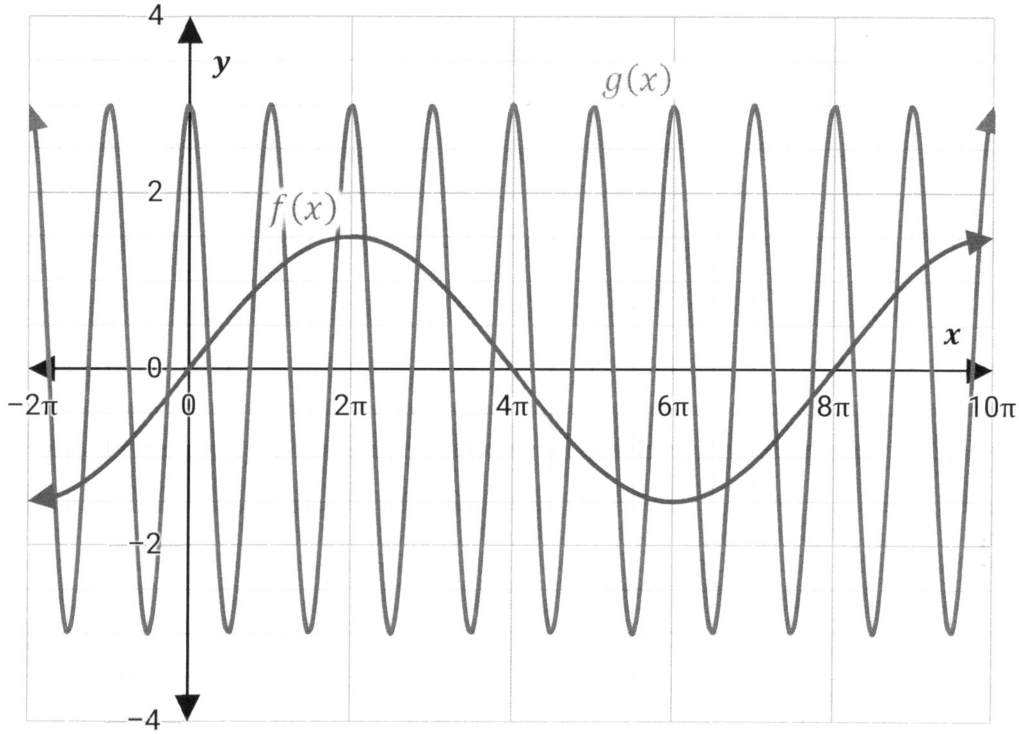

58. Which of the following statements is true?

a. The period of $f(x)$ is 2π.
b. The amplitude of the graph of $g(x)$ is 3.
c. $-1 < b_1 < 0$
d. $b_2 = \pi$

59. Identical rugs are offered for sale at two local shops and one online retailer, designated Stores A, B, and C, respectively. The rug's regular sales price is \$296 at Store A, \$220 at Store B, and \$198.00 at Store C. Stores A and B collect 8% in sales tax on any after-discount price, while Store C collects no tax but charges a \$35 shipping fee. A buyer has a 30% off coupon for Store A and a \$10 off coupon for Store B. Which of these lists the stores in order of lowest to highest final sales price after all discounts, taxes, and fees are applied?

a. Store A, Store B, Store C
b. Store B, Store C, Store A
c. Store C, Store A, Store B
d. Store C, Store B, Store A

60. If 1 inch on a map represents 25 feet, how many yards apart are two points if the distance between the points on the map is 12 inches?

a. 600
b. 300
c. 100
d. 12

61. The test scores of 250 students are normally distributed with a mean score of 84 and a standard deviation of 7. In a normal distribution, approximately 68% of values are within one standard deviation of the mean. About how many students scored 91 or higher?

a. 16
b. 40
c. 88
d. 102

62. Lucy has $25 and needs to buy pens, highlighters, and notebooks. Each pack of pens costs $4. Each pack of highlighters costs $5. Each notebook costs $1.50. Which of the following inequalities may be used to find the combinations of pens, highlighters, and notebooks that she may purchase?

a. $4p + 5h + 1.5n > 25$
b. $4p + 5h + 1.5n < 25$
c. $4p + 5h + 1.5n \leq 25$
d. $4p + 5h + 1.5n \geq 25$

63. Approximate the area A under the curve from $x = 0$ to $x = 10$ by using a Riemann sum with $\Delta x = 1$.

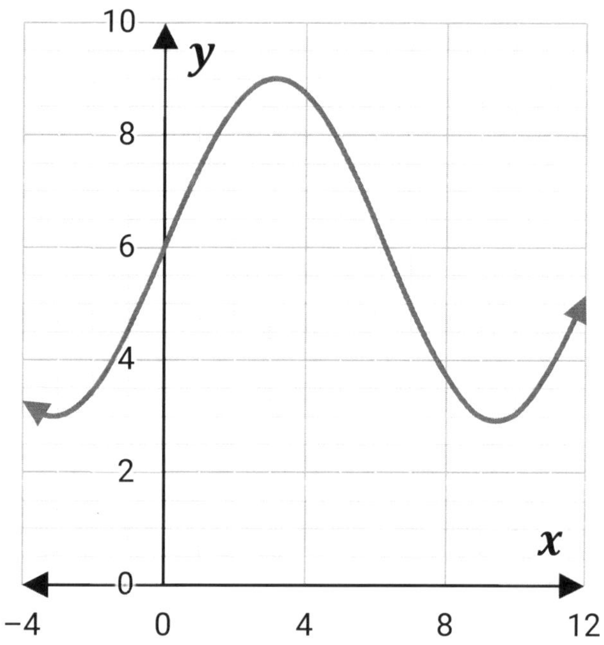

a. $59 < A < 62.25$
b. $62.25 < A < 63$
c. $62.75 < A < 65.75$
d. $65.75 < A < 68$

64. Express the area of the given triangle as a function of x.

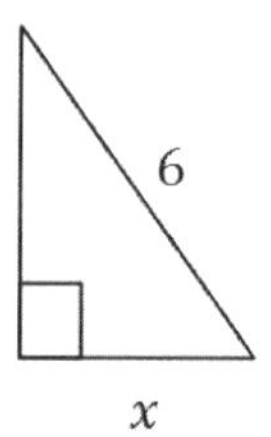

a. $A(x) = 3x$
b. $A(x) = \frac{x\sqrt{36-x^2}}{2}$
c. $A(x) = \frac{x^2}{2}$
d. $A(x) = 18 - \frac{x^2}{2}$

65. The path of a ball thrown into the air is modeled by the first quadrant graph of the equation $h(t) = -18t^2 + 72t + 4$, where $h(t)$ is the height of the ball in feet and t is time in seconds after the ball is thrown. What is the average rate of change in the ball's height with respect to time over the interval $[0, 3]$?

a. 0 feet/second
b. 6 feet/second
c. 18 feet/second
d. 24 feet/second

66. Calculate: $\int 4x^3e^{x^4}\,dx$

a. $e^{4x^3} + C$
b. $e^{x^4} + C$
c. $4x^3e^{4x^3} + C$
d. $\ln x^4 + C$

67. Lex charges $25 to mow a lawn. He spends $80 a week on fuel for his lawn mower. Which equation can be used to model this situation, where x is the number of lawns Lex mows in one week and y is the total amount of money that he makes in one week?

a. $x = 25y - 80$
b. $x = 80y - 25$
c. $y = 25x - 80$
d. $y = 80x - 25$

68. For which of these does a rotation of 120° about the center of the polygon map the polygon onto itself?

a. Square
b. Regular hexagon
c. Regular octagon
d. Regular decagon

69. Which of these graphs is representative of the data set shown below?

Stem	Leaf
1	2 6 6 8 9
2	2 3 6
3	0 1 4 4 5 7
4	2 2 2 4 5 9

KEY: $2|123 = 21, 22, 23$

a.

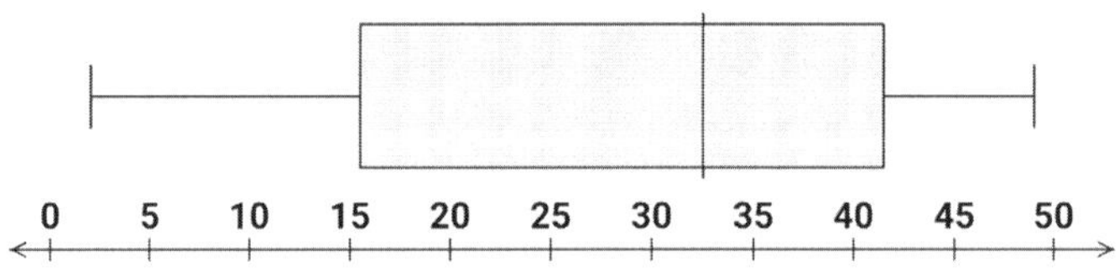

b.

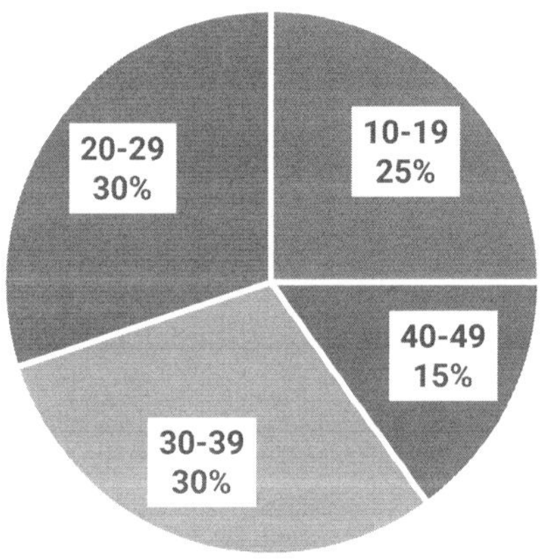

c.

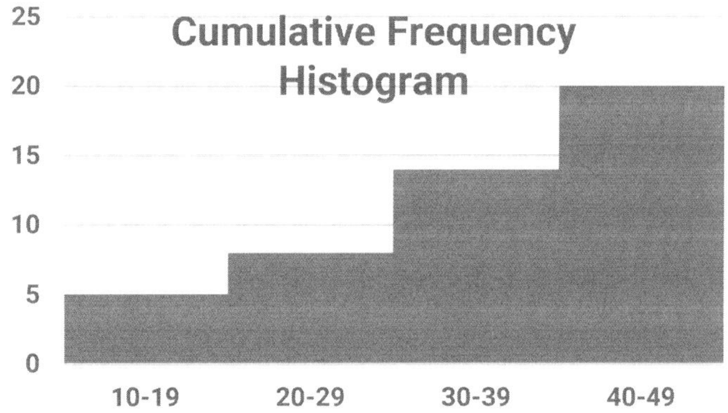

d.

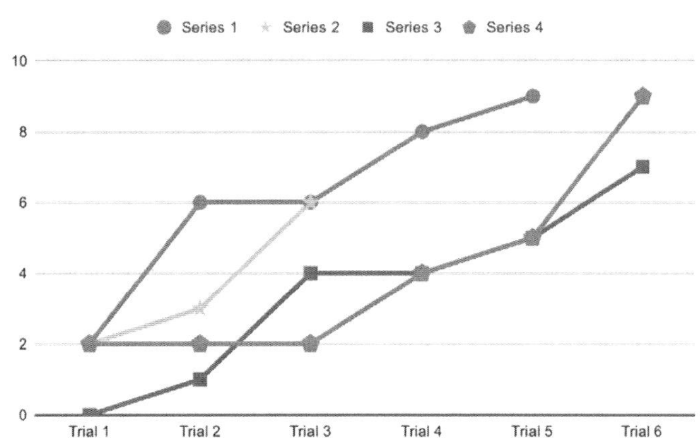

70. What is the value of b when $f(g(b)) = -6$, if $f(x)$ and $g(x)$ are inverse functions?

a. -6
b. $-\frac{1}{6}$
c. $\frac{1}{6}$
d. 6

71. Expand the following expression: $(2x - 20)(5x + 10)$

a. $10x^2 - 80x - 200$
b. $70x - 200$
c. $10x^2 - 80x + 200$
d. $10x^2 - 120x - 200$

72. Solve $x^4 + 64 = 20x^2$.

a. $x = \{2, 4\}$
b. $x = \{-4, -2, 2, 4\}$
c. $x = \{2i, 4i\}$
d. $x = \{-4i, -2i, 2i, 4i\}$

73. A music appreciation class includes 10 six-year-olds, 9 seven-year-olds, 13 eight-year-olds, 10 nine-year-olds, and 14 ten-year-olds. If a student is randomly selected to demonstrate an instrument, what is the probability that he or she is at least nine years old?

a. $\frac{37}{56}$
b. $\frac{22}{63}$
c. $\frac{4}{7}$
d. $\frac{3}{7}$

Refer to the following for question 74:

Below are graphed functions $f(x) = a_1 \sin(b_1 x)$ and $g(x) = a_2 \cos(b_2 x)$, where a_1 and a_2 are integers, and b_1 and b_2 are positive rational numbers.

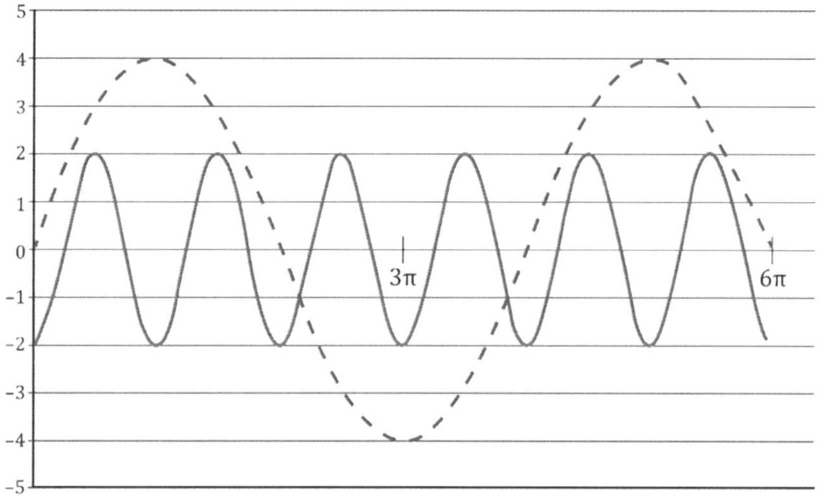

74. Which of the following statements is true?

a. $0 < a_2 < a_1$
b. $a_2 < 0 < a_1$
c. $0 < a_1 < a_2$
d. $a_2 < a_1 < 0$

75. Which of these is the equation graphed below?

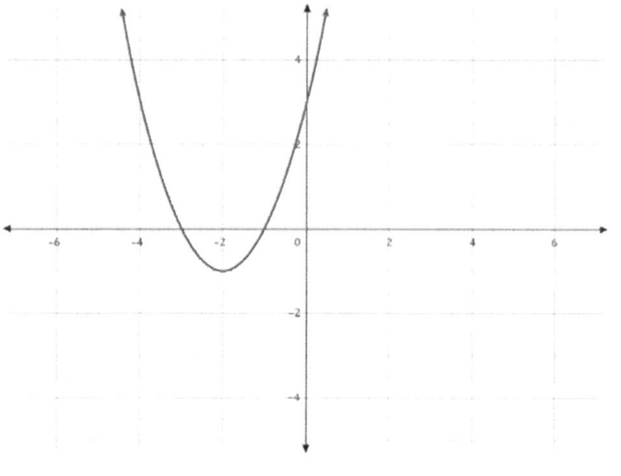

a. $y = x^2 + 4x + 3$
b. $y = x^2 - 2x - 1$
c. $y = 2x^2 + 4x + 1$
d. $y = \frac{1}{2}x^2 - 2x + 3$

76. Solve the system of equations.

$$\begin{cases} 3x - y + 2z = 2 \\ -x + 3y - z = 6 \\ 2x + 2y - z = 0 \end{cases}$$

a. $(1, 3, -2)$
b. $(-1, 3, 4)$
c. $(-\frac{1}{2}, -2, 6)$
d. No solution

77. A triangle with vertices $A(-4, 2)$, $B(-1, 3)$, and $C(-5, 7)$ is reflected across $y = -x + 1$ to give $\Delta A'B'C'$, which is subsequently reflected across the y-axis to give $\Delta A''B''C''$. Which of these statements is true?

a. A 90° rotation of ΔABC about (0,1) gives $\Delta A''B''C''$.
b. A reflection of ΔABC about the x-axis gives $\Delta A''B''C''$.
c. A 270° rotation of ΔABC about (0,1) gives $\Delta A''B''C''$.
d. A translation of ΔABC one unit down gives $\Delta A''B''C''$.

78. Ben is purchasing notebooks and boxes of pencils for a class he is teaching. Notebooks cost \$1 each and pencils cost \$3 per box. If the x-axis represents boxes of pencils, the y-axis represents notebooks, and Ben can spend a maximum of \$30, which of the following graphs shows the number of notebooks and pencils Ben can purchase?

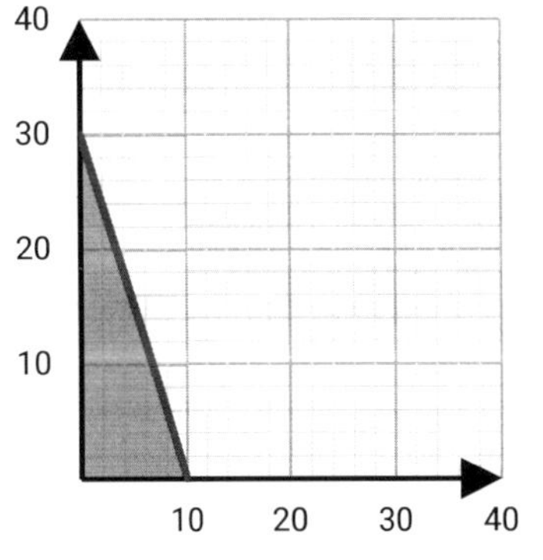

a.

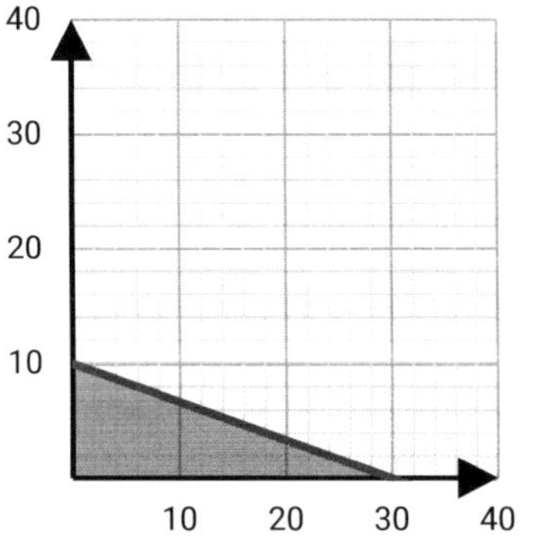

c.

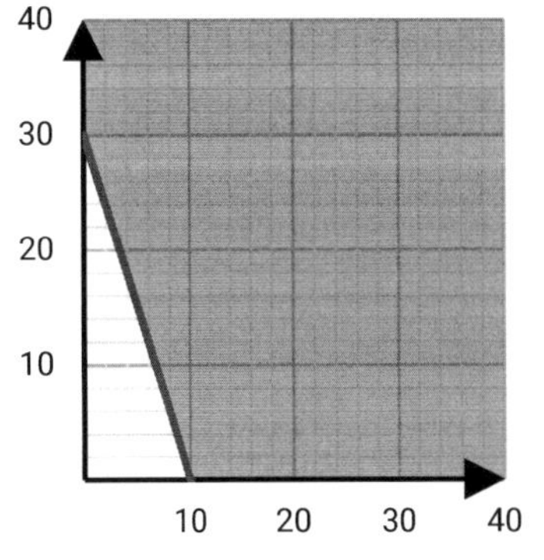

b.

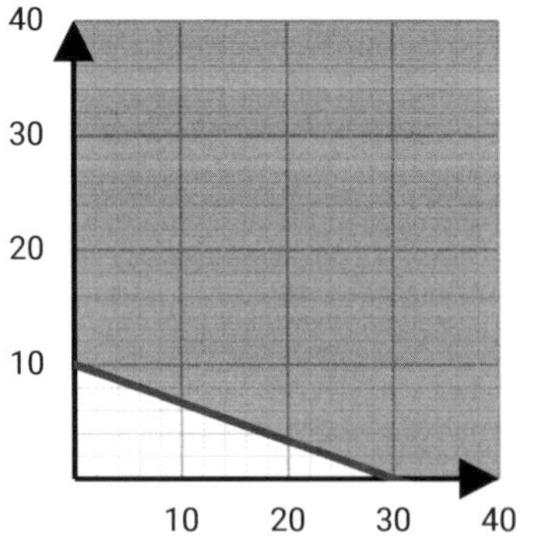

d.

79. Will needed his dinner to include at least 50 grams of protein, so he wanted to make sure he was eating enough chicken. He recalled that chicken has approximately 25 grams of protein in a 4-oz serving. He didn't have a scale that weighed ounces, but he had a 5-lb bag of flour that he planned to divide into equal portions to approximate the weight of chicken he needed, so that he could compare the weight of the flour to the chicken. Which of the following shows the calculation for the number of portions Will must divide the flour into?

a. $50 \times \frac{4}{25} \times \frac{1}{16} \times 5$
b. $25 \times 4 \times \frac{1}{16} \times \frac{1}{5}$
c. $1 \times 5 \times 16 \times \frac{25}{4} \times \frac{1}{50}$
d. $\frac{25}{4} \times \frac{16}{1} \times \frac{1}{5} \times 50$

80. Given: $f(x) = 10^x$. If $f(x) = 3$, which of these approximates x?

a. 100,000
b. 100
c. 0.5
d. 0.1

81. A small company is divided into three departments, as shown. Two individuals are chosen at random to attend a conference. What is the approximate probability that two women from the same department will be chosen?

	Department 1	Department 2	Department 3
Women	12	28	16
Men	18	14	15

a. 8.6%
b. 10.7%
c. 11.2%
d. 13.8%

82. Jen sells honey from her beehive through two local grocery stores, as well as offering it online. The two local stores (Store A and Store B) charge \$10.50 and \$11.00 per pint, respectively. Jen receives 80% of the revenue from the local stores. She charges \$6.75 per pint plus a \$2.50 shipping fee for online shoppers (Store C). During a holiday, Store A offers a sale price of 25% off. Store B offers a coupon for \$1.50 off. Jen offers a deal for free shipping. Which of the following lists the stores in order from lowest revenue to highest revenue that Jen receives during the holiday sale after all discounts and fees are applied?

a. Store A, Store C, Store B
b. Store B, Store C, Store A
c. Store C, Store A, Store B
d. Store C, Store B, Store A

83. Solve $5x^2 - 4x = -2$.

a. $x = \frac{2 \pm \sqrt{14}i}{5}$
b. $x = \pm i\sqrt{24}$
c. $x = \pm \frac{2\sqrt{2}i}{5}$
d. $x = \frac{2 \pm i\sqrt{6}}{5}$

84. A cube inscribed in a sphere has a volume of 3.375 cubic units. What is the volume of the sphere in cubic units?

a. $3\pi\sqrt{3}$
b. $\frac{9\pi\sqrt{3}}{4}$
c. $\frac{9\pi\sqrt{3}}{16}$
d. $\frac{27\pi\sqrt{3}}{16}$

85. The ratio of revenue of new car sales to used car sales at the car lot is 3 : 5. If the total revenue of car sales was $287,400 last month, what was the total revenue of the used car sales?

a. $107,775
b. $179,625
c. $192,450
d. $204,500

86. Lynn picked two tomatoes out of her garden the first week they began producing. For each subsequent week, she picked three times as many as the week before, while the plants were in season. Which of the following equations represents the amount she saved during the nth week?

a. $a_n = 2 + 3^n$
b. $a_n = 2 \times 3^{n-1}$
c. $a_n = 2 \times 3^n$
d. $a_n = 3n - 2$

87. Find the area A of the finite region between the graphs of $y = x - 3$ and $y = x^2 - 2x - 7$.

a. 7
b. $\frac{56}{3}$
c. $\frac{125}{6}$
d. 12

88. A weight suspended on a spring is at its equilibrium point 3.5 inches above the top of a table. When the weight is pulled down 3 inches, it bounces above the equilibrium point and returns to the point from which it was released in 1.5 seconds. Which of these can be used to model the weight's height *h* above the table as a function of time *t* in seconds?

a. $h = 3\cos(\pi t) + 0.5$
b. $h = -3\cos\left(\frac{4}{3}\pi t\right) + 3.5$
c. $h = -3\sin(2\pi t) + 0.5$
d. $h = 3\cos\left(\frac{2}{3}\pi t\right) + 3.5$

89. Natasha designs a square pyramidal tent for her children. Each of the sides of the square base measures *x* ft, and the tent's height is *h* feet. If Natasha were to increase by 1 ft the length of each side of the base, how much more interior space would the tent have?

a. $\frac{x^2h+2xh+h}{3}$ ft^3
b. $\frac{2xh+h}{3}$ ft^3
c. $\frac{x^2h+3}{3}$ ft^3
d. 1 ft^3

90. Jodi made a sum of money yesterday at a bake sale. She spent half of the money to buy more ingredients for next week's bake sale and then spent $12 to go to the movies. Jodi has $17 remaining. How much did she make yesterday at the bake sale?

a. $36
b. $41
c. $46
d. $58

Answer Key and Explanations for Test #2

1. D: To find the probability, we count the number of evens that were rolled, divided by the number of total rolls.

$$\frac{0 + 12 + 20(2) + 18(3)}{50(3)} = \frac{106}{150} = \frac{53}{75} \approx 0.707$$

Therefore, the approximate probability of a single roll being even is 0.707.

2. B: To simplify the inequality $x^2 + 2x \geq x + 6$, we can first move all the terms to the left-hand side.

$$x^2 + 2x - x - 6 \geq 0$$
$$x^2 + x - 6 \geq 0$$

We can now factor the left-hand side. Since the leading coefficient is 1, one way to do this is to look for two numbers that add to the coefficient of x (1) and multiply to the constant term (–6). The two numbers that qualify are –2 and 3, so $x^2 + x - 6 = (x - 2)(x + 3)$.

$$(x - 2)(x + 3) \geq 0$$

We know the dividing points for the regions that do and do not satisfy the inequality are then at $x - 2 = 0$ and at $x + 3 = 0$, that is at $x = 2$ and at $x = -3$. Consider the sign in each region: when $x < -3$, then $x - 2$ and $x + 3$ are both negative, and their product is positive. When $-3 < x < 2$, then $x - 2$ is negative and $x + 3$ is positive, so their product is negative. When $x > 2$, then then $x - 2$ and $x + 3$ are both positive, and their product is positive: $(x - 2)(x + 3) \geq 0$ when $x \leq -3$ or $x \geq 2$.

3. D: "The square of three times the sum of a and six is fourteen more than a" is represented by the equation $[3(a + 6)]^2 = a + 14$. Solve for a.

$$\begin{aligned}[3a + 18]^2 &= a + 14\\ 9a^2 + 108a + 324 &= a + 14\\ 9a^2 + 107a + 310 &= 0\\ (a + 5)(9a + 62) &= 0\\ a &= -5, -\frac{62}{9}\end{aligned}$$

So, –5 is a possible value of a.

4. D: First, apply the laws of exponents to simplify the expression on the left. Then, add the two fractions.

$\frac{(x^2y^{-3})(4xy)^2}{16x^4y^4} + \frac{3}{2xy}$	Write out the original expression.
$\frac{(x^2y^{-3})(16x^2y^2)}{16x^4y^4} + \frac{3}{2xy}$	Simplify the squared term in the left fraction's numerator.
$\frac{16x^4y^{-1}}{16x^4y^4} + \frac{3}{2xy}$	Multiply the two monomials in the left fraction's numerator using the exponent rule $x^m \cdot x^n = x^{m+n}$.

$\frac{1}{y^5} + \frac{3}{2xy}$	Simplify the left fraction using the exponent rule $\frac{x^m}{x^n} = x^{m-n}$ and the rule $x^{-n} = \frac{1}{x^n}$.
$\frac{1}{y^5} \cdot \frac{2x}{2x} + \frac{3}{2xy} \cdot \frac{y^4}{y^4}$	Create common denominators between the two fractions by multiplying them each by a factor of 1.
$\frac{2x}{2xy^5} + \frac{3y^4}{2xy^5}$	Simplify the multiplication.
$\frac{2x + 3y^4}{2xy^5}$	Add the two fractions.

5. C: When you have a ratio, you can find the fraction that each part of the ratio is of the whole by dividing a part by the sum of the parts. Since the ratio of wages and benefits to other costs is 2: 3, the amount of money spent on wages and benefits is $\frac{2}{2+3} = \frac{2}{5}$ of total operational costs.

$$\frac{2}{5} \times \$130{,}000 = \$52{,}000$$

6. A: First, multiply the numerator and denominator by the denominator's conjugate, $3 + 2i$. Then, simplify the result and write the answer in the form $a + bi$. Recall, $i^2 = -1$.

$$\begin{aligned} \frac{4+i}{3-2i} \times \frac{3+2i}{3+2i} &= \frac{12 + 8i + 3i + 2i^2}{9 - 4i^2} \\ &= \frac{12 + 11i - 2}{9 + 4} \\ &= \frac{10 + 11i}{13} \\ &= \frac{10}{13} + \frac{11}{13}i \end{aligned}$$

7. B: To find the derivative, use the chain rule $\left(\frac{dy}{dx} = \frac{dy}{du} \cdot \frac{du}{dx}\right)$.

$$y = e^{2x^4+2}$$

Let $u = 2x^4 + 2$ and find $\frac{du}{dx}$.

$$\frac{du}{dx} = 8x^3$$

Next, let $y = e^u$ and find $\frac{dy}{du}$.

$$\frac{dy}{du} = e^u$$

Finally, use the chain rule to find $\frac{dy}{dx}$.

$$\frac{dy}{dx} = e^{2x^4+2} \cdot 8x^3 = (8x^3)e^{2x^4+2}$$

8. B: The coterminal angle for $-\frac{7\pi}{6}$ is $-\frac{7\pi}{6} + 2\pi = \frac{5\pi}{6}$. Also, remember that tangent of an angle can be found by dividing the sine of the angle by the cosine of the angle.

$$\tan\left(-\frac{7\pi}{6}\right) = \tan\left(\frac{5\pi}{6}\right) = \frac{\sin\left(\frac{5\pi}{6}\right)}{\cos\left(\frac{5\pi}{6}\right)}$$

From the unit circle, the values of $\sin\left(\frac{5\pi}{6}\right)$ and $\cos\left(\frac{5\pi}{6}\right)$ are $\frac{1}{2}$ and $-\frac{\sqrt{3}}{2}$, respectively. Substitute these values and simplify.

$$\tan\left(-\frac{7\pi}{6}\right) = \frac{\frac{1}{2}}{-\frac{\sqrt{3}}{2}} = \frac{1}{2} \div \left(-\frac{\sqrt{3}}{2}\right) = \frac{1}{2} \times \left(-\frac{2}{\sqrt{3}}\right) = -\frac{1}{\sqrt{3}} = -\frac{1 \times \sqrt{3}}{\sqrt{3} \times \sqrt{3}} = -\frac{\sqrt{3}}{3}$$

Therefore, the exact value of $\tan(-\frac{7\pi}{6})$ is $-\frac{\sqrt{3}}{3}$.

9. D: Consider each answer choice. The x-intercept is the point at which $f(x) = 0$. When $0 = \log_b x$, $b^0 = x$; since $b^0 = 1$, the x-intercept of $f(x) = \log_b x$ is always 1. If $f(x) = \log_b x$ and $x = b$, then $f(x) = \log_b b$, which is, by definition, 1 ($b^1 = b$). The statement $f(x) < 0$ is true only for x-values between 0 and 1. Choice D states, "If $g(x) = x^b$, the graph of $f(x)$ is symmetric to the graph of $g(x)$ with respect to $y = x$." This is a false statement. On the other hand, if $g(x) = b^x$, then $f(x)$ and $g(x)$ are inverse functions and are therefore symmetric with respect to $y = x$.

10. B: To solve, start by dropping the parentheses and grouping like terms.

$$3x^2 + x + 3 + 8x^2 + 5x + 16$$
$$(3x^2 + 8x^2) + (x + 5x) + (3 + 16)$$

Then, combine like terms.

$$11x^2 + 6x + 19$$

11. A: The slope of the line tangent to the graph of a function f at $x = a$ is $f'(a)$. Start by finding the derivative of $f(x)$.

$$f(x) = \frac{2}{3}x^2 + 4$$
$$f'(x) = 2\left(\frac{2}{3}\right)x^{(2-1)} + 0$$
$$f'(x) = \frac{4}{3}x$$

So, the slope at $x = -3$ is $f'(-3) = \frac{4}{3}(-3) = -4$.

12. C: The percentage of students taking Java or Creative Writing is $25\% + 21\% = 46\%$. The percentage of students in electives who are male is $\frac{92}{200} \times 100\% = 46\%$. So, the two quantities are equal.

13. A: The velocity v of the ball at any time t is the slope of the line tangent to the graph of h at time t. The slope of a line tangent to the curve $h(t) = -15t^2 + 56t + 3.5$ is the same as h'.

$$h'(t) = v(t) = -30t + 56$$

When $t = 1.5$, the velocity of the ball is $-30(1.5) + 56 = 11$. The velocity is positive because the slope of the tangent line at $t = 1.5$ is positive. Velocity has both magnitude and direction, so a velocity of 11 means that the velocity is 11 ft/s upward.

14. B: If l and w represent the length and width of the enclosed area, its perimeter is equal to $2l + 2w$. Since the fence is positioned x feet from the lot's edges on each side, the perimeter of the original pen is $2(l + 2x) + 2(w + 2x)$. Since the amount of money saved by fencing the smaller area is $648, and since the fencing material costs $9 per linear foot, 72 fewer feet of material are used to fence around the cattle pen than would have been used to fence around the original plan. This can be expressed as the following equation.

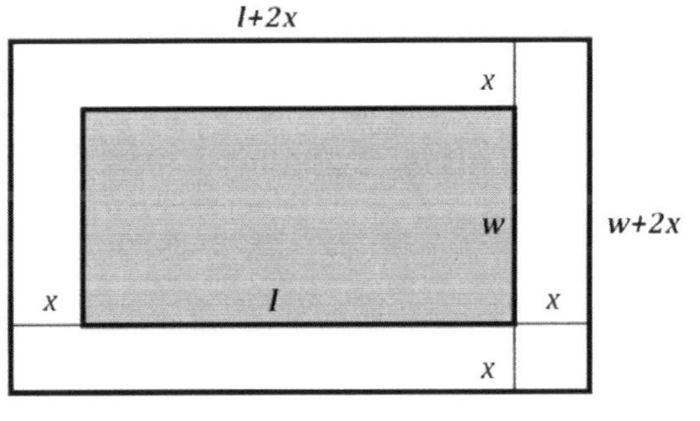

$$\begin{aligned} 2(l + 2x) + 2(w + 2x) - (2l + 2w) &= 72 \\ 2l + 4x + 2w + 4x - 2l - 2w &= 72 \\ 8x &= 72 \\ x &= 9 \text{ ft} \end{aligned}$$

The difference in the area of the lot and the enclosed space is 764 yd^2, which is the same as 6,876 ft^2. So, $(l + 2x)(w + 2x) - lw = 6{,}876$. Substituting 9 for x, and solving for $l + w$, we get the following equations.

$$\begin{aligned} (l + 18)(w + 18) - lw &= 6{,}876 \\ lw + 18l + 18w + 324 - lw &= 6{,}876 \\ 18l + 18w &= 6{,}552 \\ 18(l + w) &= 6{,}552 \\ l + w &= 364 \text{ ft} \end{aligned}$$

Therefore, the perimeter of the enclosed space, $2(l + w)$, is $2(364) = 728$ ft. The cost of 728 ft of fencing is $728 \times \$9 = \$6{,}552$.

15. C: Evaluate $\frac{x^3+3x^2-x-3}{x^2-9}$ at $x = -3$.

$$\frac{(-3)^3 + 3(-3)^2 - (-3) - 3}{(-3)^2 - 9} = \frac{-27 + 3(9) + 3 - 3}{9 - 9} = \frac{-27 + 27 + 3 - 3}{9 - 9} = \frac{0}{0}$$

Since evaluating $\frac{x^3+3x^2-x-3}{x^2-9}$ at $x = -3$ produces a fraction with a zero denominator, simplify the polynomial expression before evaluating the limit.

Simplify the polynomial expression:

$$\frac{x^3 + 3x^2 - x - 3}{x^2 - 9}$$

$$\frac{x^2(x + 3) - 1(x + 3)}{(x + 3)(x - 3)}$$ Factor out $(x + 3)$ from the first two terms and the 3rd and 4th terms in the numerator, and factor the denominator.

$$\frac{(x + 3)(x^2 - 1)}{(x + 3)(x - 3)}$$ Factor out $(x + 3)$ completely in the numerator.

$$\frac{(x + 1)(x - 1)}{x - 3}$$ Cancel the common $(x + 3)$ terms in the numerator and denominator.

Now, evaluate the limit.

$$\lim_{x \to -3} \frac{(x + 1)(x - 1)}{x - 3}$$

$$\frac{(-3 + 1)(-3 - 1)}{-3 - 3}$$ Substitute –3 into the expression for x.

$$\frac{8}{-6}$$ Simplify the numerator and denominator.

$$-\frac{4}{3}$$ Simplify the fraction.

16. B: Start by distributing each coefficient across the parentheses. Next add the complex binomials. Complex numbers have a real part, *a,* and an imaginary part, *b*, and are usually written as $a + bi$. When adding imaginary numbers, add the real parts and the imaginary parts separately.

$$\begin{aligned} -2(2+6i) - 4(2-3i) &= -4 - 12i - 8 - (-12i) \\ &= (-4-8) + (-12i + 12i) \\ &= -12 \end{aligned}$$

17. D: Solve the inequality using inverse operations. Start by adding 9 to both sides of the inequality.

$$\begin{aligned} 2|x+3| - 9 &\geq -1 \\ 2|x+3| &\geq 8 \end{aligned}$$

Then, divide both sides by 2.

$$|x+3| \geq 4$$

From here, separate the inequality into two inequalities to get rid of the absolute value, and solve each inequality.

$$\begin{aligned} x + 3 &\geq 4 \\ x &\geq 1 \end{aligned}$$

$$\begin{aligned} -(x+3) &\geq 4 \\ x + 3 &\leq -4 \\ x &\leq -7 \end{aligned}$$

Therefore, the solution to the inequality is $x \leq -7$ or $x \geq 1$.

18. D: The sum of two vectors is equal to the sum of their components.

$$v + w = \big((-2+0), (-3+4)\big) = (-2,1)$$

To multiply a vector by a scalar, multiply each component by that scalar.

$$\frac{1}{2}(-2,1) = \left(-2 \times \frac{1}{2}, 1 \times \frac{1}{2}\right) = \left(-1, \frac{1}{2}\right)$$

19. A: 20 of the 38 sophomores taking an elective are male. The probability that a male is chosen is $\frac{\text{number of male sophomores}}{\text{number of sophomores}} = \frac{20}{38} \approx 0.53$.

20. C: First, add the matrices in parentheses, then multiply the resulting matrices together:

$$\begin{aligned} [1 \quad -3 \quad 2]\begin{bmatrix} (-3+3) \\ (2+4) \\ (1-2) \end{bmatrix} &= [1 \quad -3 \quad 2]\begin{bmatrix} 0 \\ 6 \\ -1 \end{bmatrix} \\ &= [(1)(0) + (-3)(6) + (2)(-1)] \\ &= [-20] \end{aligned}$$

Note that the product of a 1×3 matrix and a 3×1 matrix, in that order, is a 1×1 matrix. If the order was reversed, the product would be a 3×3 matrix.

21. A: If the distance is 5 cm on the map, then the actual distance is $5 \times 15 = 75$ m. To find x, use the Pythagorean theorem.

$$x^2 + (x + 15)^2 = (75)^2$$
$$x^2 + x^2 + 30x + 225 = 5{,}625$$
$$2x^2 + 30x - 5{,}400 = 0$$
$$2(x^2 + 15x - 2{,}700) = 0$$
$$2(x - 45)(x + 60) = 0$$
$$x = 45 \quad x = -60$$

Since x represents a distance in this situation, use the positive value. Since $x = 45$, $x + 15 = 60$. Milly walks a total of $45 + 60 = 105$ m to get to the store.

22. D: First, find out what the total temperature decrease will be after 4 minutes.

$$2 \times 4 = 8$$

The temperature will have decreased by 8 degrees after 4 minutes. Then, subtract this from the original temperature.

$$98 - 8 = 90$$

The temperature of the coffee is 90 degrees after 4 minutes.

23. D: Let b represent the base of the triangle. The height h of the triangle is the altitude drawn from the vertex opposite of b to side b.

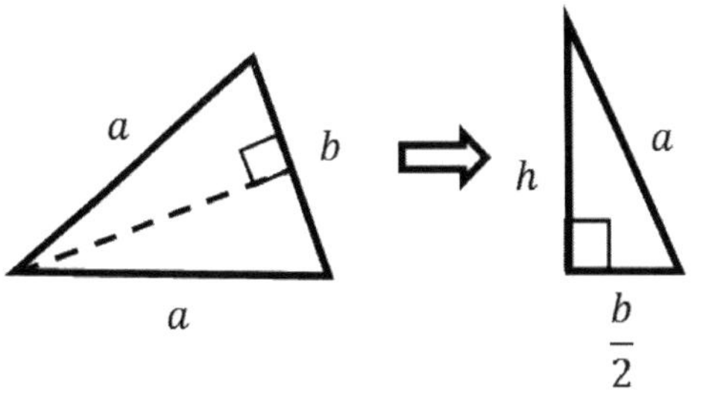

The height of the triangle can be found in terms of a and b by using the Pythagorean theorem.

$$h^2 + \left(\frac{b}{2}\right)^2 = a^2$$
$$h = \sqrt{a^2 - \frac{b^2}{4}}$$
$$h = \sqrt{\frac{4a^2 - b^2}{4}}$$
$$h = \frac{\sqrt{4a^2 - b^2}}{2}$$

The area of a triangle is $A = \frac{1}{2}bh$, so $A = \frac{1}{2}b\left(\frac{\sqrt{4a^2-b^2}}{2}\right) = \frac{b\sqrt{4a^2-b^2}}{4}$.

24. A: Start by determining which values of x are not possible solutions. For this equation, x cannot equal -1 or -7 because these would result in denominator values of 0.

Then, solve the equation as normal.

$$\frac{x+2}{x+1} = \frac{x+9}{x+7} + \frac{2}{x+1}$$

$$\frac{x}{x+1} = \frac{x+9}{x+7}$$ Subtract $\frac{2}{x+1}$ from both sides of the equation.

$$(x)(x+7) = (x+9)(x+1)$$ Cross multiply to eliminate the fractions.

$$x^2 + 7x = x^2 + 10x + 9$$ Multiply the polynomials.

$$7x = 10x + 9$$ Subtract x^2 from both sides of the equation

$$-3x = 9$$ Subtract $10x$ from both sides of the equation.

$$x = -3$$ Divide both sides of the equation by -3.

Since -3 is not one of the values x cannot be equal to, our answer is $x = -3$.

25. D: The acceleration a of an object at time t is the derivative of the velocity v of the object with respect to time t. The velocity v is the derivative of the position s of the object with respect to time t. So, given the velocity of an object at time t, $s(t)$ can be found by taking the integral of the $v(t)$, and $a(t)$ can be found by taking the derivative of $v(t)$.

$$\begin{aligned} s(t) &= \int v(t)dt \\ &= \int (10t - t^2)dt \\ &= 5t^2 - \frac{1}{3}t^3 + C \end{aligned}$$

Since the position of the car at time 0 is 0:

$$\begin{aligned} 0 &= s(0) \\ 0 &= 5(0)^2 - \frac{1}{3}(0)^3 + C \\ 0 &= 0 - 0 + C \\ 0 &= C \end{aligned}$$

Therefore, $s(t) = 5t^2 - \frac{1}{3}t^3$.

The acceleration at time t is $a(t) = v'(t) = 10 - 2t$.

Find the time at which the acceleration is equal to 0.

$$\begin{aligned} 0 &= 10 - 2t \\ -10 &= -2t \\ 5 &= t \end{aligned}$$

Then, find $s(5)$ to find the position of the car when the velocity is 0.

$$s(5) = 5(5)^2 - \frac{1}{3}(5)^3 = 125 - \frac{125}{3} = \frac{250}{3}$$

26. C: Sketch a diagram and label the known segments. Use the property that two segments are congruent when they originate from the same point outside of a circle and are tangent to the circle. The point of tangency of $\overline{CD}$ divides the segment into two pieces measuring 4 and 4. The point of tangency of $\overline{BC}$ divides the segment into two pieces measuring 4 and 8; the point of tangency of $\overline{AB}$ divides the segment into two pieces measuring 2 and 8. Finally, the point of tangency of $\overline{AD}$ divides the segment into two pieces measuring 2 and 4. Therefore, $\overline{AD} = 2 + 4 = 6$.

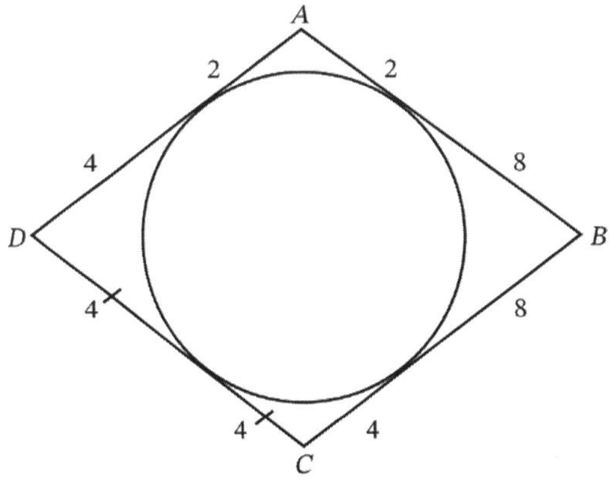

27. A: The equation of the circle is given in general form. When the equation is written in the standard form $(x-h)^2 + (y-k)^2 = r^2$, where (h,k) is the center of the circle and r is the radius of the circle, the radius is easy to determine. Write the equation in standard form by completing the square for x and y.

$$x^2 - 10x + y^2 + 8y = -29$$
$$(x^2 - 10x + 25) + (y^2 + 8y + 16) = -29 + 25 + 16$$
$$(x-5)^2 + (y+4)^2 = 12$$

Since $r^2 = 12$, and since r must be a positive number, $r = \sqrt{12} = 2\sqrt{3}$.

28. D: If x is the cost of the pen, then, $2x$ is the cost of the book and $4x$ is the cost of the calculator. Vivian has spent $x + 2x + 4x$, or $7x$. She started with \$50 and had \$15 left, so $\$50 - 7x = \$15$. Solving for x, $x = \frac{\$50-\$15}{7} = \frac{\$35}{7} = \$5$, and the cost of the calculator was $4x = 4(\$5) = \$20$.

29. B: To graph a piecewise function, graph each part of the function for the given domain values. In this case, graph the function $4 - x^2$ for the x-values $x < 0$, graph the function $4 - 2x$ for the values $0 \le x < 2$, and graph the function $7 - x$ for the values $x \ge 2$. By inspection of the graph, we see that there is no discontinuity at $x = 0$, because the two functions on either side of $x = 0$ meet at 4. There is a discontinuity at $x = 2$, because the function to the left of $x = 2$ approaches 0, while the function to the right of $x = 2$ is equal to 5 at the point $x = 2$. Also, the maximum value of the function is $f(2) = 5$.

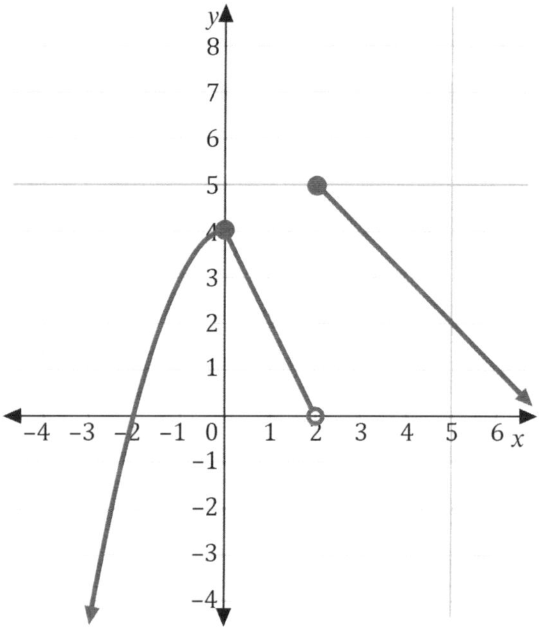

30. B: On the unit circle, $\sin\theta = \frac{\sqrt{2}}{2}$ when $\theta = \frac{\pi}{4}$ and when $\theta = \frac{3\pi}{4}$. Only $\frac{3\pi}{4}$ fits the condition $\frac{\pi}{2} < \theta < \pi$, so $\theta = \frac{3\pi}{4}$.

31. C: Use trigonometric identities to simplify.

$\cos\theta\cot\theta$	Write out the original expression.
$\cos\theta \times \frac{\cos\theta}{\sin\theta}$	Convert $\cot\theta$ to its identity $\frac{\cos\theta}{\sin\theta}$.
$\frac{\cos^2\theta}{\sin\theta}$	Multiply the two terms.
$\frac{1-\sin^2\theta}{\sin\theta}$	Convert $\cos^2\theta$ to its identity $1-\sin^2\theta$.
$\frac{1}{\sin\theta} - \frac{\sin^2\theta}{\sin\theta}$	Split the fraction into two separate fractions.
$\frac{1}{\sin\theta} - \sin\theta$	Simplify the second term by dividing.
$\csc\theta - \sin\theta$	Convert $\frac{1}{\sin\theta}$ to $\csc\theta$.

32. A: In order for a set to be a group under operation $*$:

- The set must be closed under that operation. In other words, when the operation is performed on any two members of the set, the result must also be a member of that set.
- The set must demonstrate associativity under the operation: $a * (b * c) = (a * b) * c$

- There must exist an identity element e in the group: $a * e = e * a = a$
- For every element in the group, there must exist an inverse element in the group: $a * b = b * a = e$

Choices B and D can easily be eliminated as the correct answer because they do not contain the additive identity 0. Though choice C contains the element 0, it is not closed: for example, $-1 + -1 = -2$, so −2 must be an element of the group since it is a possible result of adding set elements together. Choice A is closed, contains the additive identity 0, and the additive inverse of each element is included in the set as well. Of course, addition is an associative operation, so the set $\{0\}$ forms a group under addition.

+	**0**
0	0

33. C: Choice C is the equation for an absolute value function. A function is a relationship in which for every element of the domain (x), there is exactly one element of the range (y). Graphically, a relationship between x and y can be identified as a function if the graph passes the vertical line test. The absolute value function passes this test.

The first relation is a parabola on its side, which fails the vertical line test for functions. A circle (choice B) also fails the vertical line test and is therefore not a function. The relation in choice D pairs two elements of the range with one of the elements of the domain, so it is also not a function.

34. A: The manufacturer wishes to minimize the surface area A of the can while keeping its volume V fixed at $1\text{ L} = 1{,}000\text{ mL} = 1{,}000\text{ cm}^3$. The formula for the surface area of a cylinder is $A = 2\pi rh + 2\pi r^2$, and the formula for volume is $V = \pi r^2 h$. To combine the two formulas into one, solve the volume formula for r or h and substitute the resulting expression into the surface area formula for r or h. The volume of the cylinder is $1{,}000\text{ cm}^3$, so $1{,}000 = \pi r^2 h \rightarrow h = \frac{1{,}000}{\pi r^2}$. Therefore, $A = 2\pi rh + 2\pi r^2 \rightarrow 2\pi r\left(\frac{1{,}000}{\pi r^2}\right) + 2\pi r^2 = \frac{2{,}000}{r} + 2\pi r^2$. Find the critical point(s) by setting the first derivative equal to zero and solving for r. Note that r represents the radius of the can and must therefore be a positive number.

$$A = 2{,}000r^{-1} + 2\pi r^2$$
$$A' = -2{,}000r^{-2} + 4\pi r$$
$$0 = -\frac{2{,}000}{r^2} + 4\pi r$$
$$\frac{2{,}000}{r^2} = 4\pi r$$
$$2{,}000 = 4\pi r^3$$
$$\sqrt[3]{\frac{2{,}000}{4\pi}} = r$$
$$5.42 \approx r$$

So, when $r \approx 5.42$ cm, the minimum surface area is obtained. When the radius of the can is 5.42 cm, its height is $h \approx \frac{1{,}000}{\pi(5.42)^2} \approx 10.84$ cm, and surface area is approximately $\frac{2{,}000}{5.42} + 2\pi(5.42)^2 \approx 553.58\text{ cm}^2$. Confirm that the surface area is greater when the radius is slightly smaller or larger than 5.42 cm. For instance, when $r = 5$ cm, the surface area is approximately 557.08 cm^2, and when $r = 6$ cm, the surface area is approximately 559.53 cm^2.

35. D: ΔADC is a right triangle with legs measuring 8 and 15 and a hypotenuse of 17. (8–15–17 is a Pythagorean triple.) ΔADC and ΔDEC are both right triangles which share vertex C. By the AA similarity theorem, $\Delta ADC \sim \Delta DEC$. Therefore, a proportion can be written and solved to find DE.

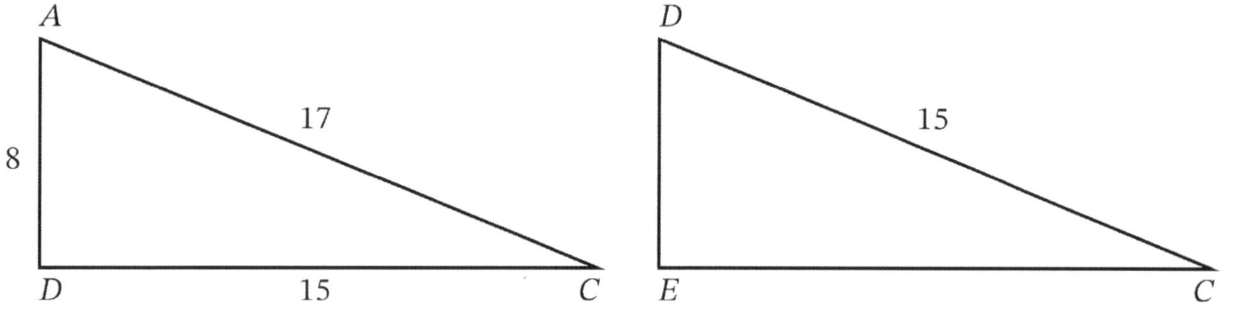

$$\frac{8}{DE} = \frac{17}{15}$$
$$17DE = 120$$
$$DE \approx 7.1$$

36. B: The trigonometric identity $\sec^2\theta = \tan^2\theta + 1$ can be used to rewrite the equation $\sec^2\theta = 2\tan\theta$ as $\tan^2\theta + 1 = 2\tan\theta$, which can then be rearranged into the form $\tan^2\theta - 2\tan\theta + 1 = 0$. Solve by factoring and using the zero-product property.

$$\tan^2\theta - 2\tan\theta + 1 = 0$$
$$(\tan\theta - 1)^2 = 0$$
$$\tan\theta - 1 = 0$$
$$\tan\theta = 1$$

Since $\tan\theta = 1$ when $\sin\theta = \cos\theta$, for $0 < \theta \le 2\pi$, $\theta = \frac{\pi}{4}$ or $\frac{5\pi}{4}$.

37. D: 75% of the data in a set is above the first quartile. Since the first quartile for this set is 73, there is a 75% chance, or a probability of 0.75, that a student chosen at random from class 2 scored above a 73.

38. A: The slope of the original line is $m = -\frac{5}{2}$. Since the new line needs to be parallel, the new slope needs to be the same as the original slope. The given point is (2,3), which is equivalent to (x_1, y_1) in the point-slope equation of $y - y_1 = m(x - x_1)$. Substitute in the new slope and given point.

$$y - 3 = -\frac{5}{2}(x - 2)$$

Distribute on the right side of the equation.

$$y - 3 = -\frac{5}{2}x + 5$$

Add 3 to both sides of the equation.

$$y = -\frac{5}{2}x + 8$$

Multiply through by 2 and move the x-value to the left to get the answer in standard form.

$$5x + 2y = 16$$

Therefore, the equation of a line parallel to $y = -\frac{5}{2}x + 2$ that passes through the point (2,3) is $5x + 2y = 16$.

39. D: Bacterial growth is exponential. Let x be the number of times the population doubles, a be the number of bacteria in the colony originally transferred into the broth, and y be the number of bacteria in the broth after x doubling times. After 1 hour, the population would have doubled three times:

$$\begin{aligned} a(2)^x &= y \\ a(2^3) &= 8 \times 10^6 \\ 8a &= 8 \times 10^6 \\ a &= 10^6 \end{aligned}$$

So, the number of bacteria originally transferred into the petri dish was 10^6. The equation for determining the number of bacteria is $y = (2^x) \times 10^6$. Since the bacteria double every twenty minutes, they go through three doubling times every hour. So, when the bacteria are allowed to grow for eight hours, they will have gone through $8 \times 3 = 24$ doubling times. When $x = 24$, $y = (2^{24}) \times 10^6 = 16{,}777{,}216 \times 10^6$, which is approximately 1.7×10^{13}.

40. C: Substitute and simplify:

$$\begin{aligned} (g \circ f)(x) &= g\big(f(x)\big) \\ &= g(3x - 2) \\ &= (3x - 2)^2 - (3x - 2) - 6 \\ &= 9x^2 - 12x + 4 - 3x + 2 - 6 \\ &= 9x^2 - 15x \end{aligned}$$

41. C: ΔABC is similar to the smaller triangle with which it shares vertex B.

$$\overline{BC} = (2x - 2) + (x + 4) = 3x + 2$$

$$\overline{AB} = 3 + 9 = 12$$

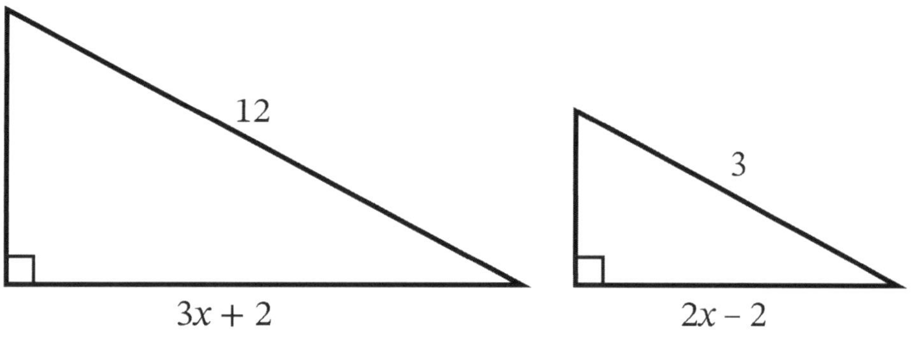

Set up a proportion and solve for x:

$$\frac{3x+2}{12} = \frac{2x-2}{3}$$
$$9x + 6 = 24x - 24$$
$$30 = 15x$$
$$x = 2$$

So, $BC = 3x + 2 = 3(2) + 2 = 8$.

42. A: First, multiply the numerator and denominator by the denominator's conjugate, $4 + 2i$. Then, simplify the result and write the answer in the form $a + bi$. Remember, $i^2 = -1$.

$$\begin{aligned}\frac{2+3i}{4-2i} \times \frac{4+2i}{4+2i} &= \frac{8+4i+12i+6i^2}{16-4i^2}\\ &= \frac{8+16i-6}{16+4}\\ &= \frac{2+16i}{20}\\ &= \frac{2}{20}+\frac{16i}{20}\\ &= \frac{1}{10}+\frac{4}{5}i\end{aligned}$$

43. C: In the figure, since the given angle is located between the two given sides, we need to use the law of cosines to solve for x. The law of cosines is $c^2 = a^2 + b^2 - 2ab\cos(C)$. If we let $a = 12$, $b = 9.5$ and $c = x$, then the law of cosines becomes $x^2 = 12^2 + 9.5^2 - 2(12)(9.5)\cos(63°)$. This simplifies to $x^2 = 130.74$. Therefore, $x = 11.4$.

44. B: The range is the spread of the data. It can be calculated for each test by subtracting the lowest test score from the highest, or it can be determined visually from the graph. The difference between the highest and lowest test scores on the Midterm is $91 - 22 = 69$ points. The range for each of the other classes is much smaller.

45. A: A function is a relation in which there is not any x-value that is mapped to more than one y-value. The only relation that represents a function is $\{(2,1), (3,-2), (6,8), (-1,-4), (4,-1)\}$.

46. C: The recursive definition of the sequence gives the first term of the series, $a_1 = -2$. The definition also defines each term in the series as the sum of the previous term and $\frac{1}{2}$. Therefore, the second term in the series is $-2 + \frac{1}{2} = -\frac{3}{2}$, the third term in the series is $-\frac{3}{2} + \frac{1}{2} = -1$, and so on.

n	a_n
1	-2
2	$-\frac{3}{2}$
3	-1

The relationship between n and a_n is linear, so the equation of the sequence can be found in the same way as the equation of a line. The value of a_n increases by $\frac{1}{2}$ each time the value of n increases by 1.

n	$\frac{n}{2}$	a_n
1	$\frac{1}{2}$	-2
2	1	$-\frac{3}{2}$
3	$\frac{3}{2}$	-1

Since the difference between $\frac{1}{2}n$ and a_n is $-\frac{5}{2}$. So, $a_n = \frac{1}{2}n - \frac{5}{2}$.

n	$\frac{n}{2} - \frac{5}{2}$	a_n
1	$\frac{1}{2} - \frac{5}{2}$	-2
2	$1 - \frac{5}{2}$	$-\frac{3}{2}$
3	$\frac{3}{2} - \frac{5}{2}$	-1

47. C: 65 of 118 volunteers under the age of 21 are male. So, the probability that a male is chosen is $\frac{\text{number of 0–20 year–old males}}{\text{number of 0–20 year–olds}} = \frac{65}{118} \approx 0.55$.

48. B: A standard result from high school geometry states that the perpendicular bisector of a chord passes through the center of the circle. Thus, two distinct perpendicular bisectors of chords intersect at the center of the circle. Therefore, this construction works except in the case that both chords share the same perpendicular bisector, which happens precisely when the chords are parallel, the special case in which the student's construction fails.

49. C: To evaluate the limit, divide the numerator and denominator by x^2 and use these properties of limits: $\lim_{x\to\infty}\frac{1}{x}=0$; the limit of a sum of terms is the sum of the limits of the terms; and the limit of a product of terms is the product of the limits of the terms.

$$\lim_{x\to\infty}\frac{4x^2+2x-1}{2x^2-3}=\lim_{x\to\infty}\frac{\frac{4x^2}{x^2}+\frac{2x}{x^2}-\frac{1}{x^2}}{\frac{2x^2}{x^2}-\frac{3}{x^2}}=\lim_{x\to\infty}\frac{4+\frac{2}{x}-\frac{1}{x^2}}{2-\frac{3}{x^2}}=\frac{4+0-0}{2+0}=\frac{4}{2}=2$$

Therefore, the limit is 2.

50. A: To find the slope of the line, use the slope formula.

$$m=\frac{y_2-y_1}{x_2-x_1}$$

Substitute $(-3,18)$ for (x_1,y_1) and $(5,2)$ for (x_2,y_2).

$$m=\frac{2-18}{5-(-3)}=\frac{2-18}{5+3}=\frac{-16}{8}=-2$$

Therefore, the slope of the line is –2.

51. B: Get as many terms as possible out from the radical and any radicals out from the denominator:

$$\begin{aligned}\sqrt{\frac{-32x^4}{75y^5}}&=\sqrt{\frac{-16x^4\cdot(2)}{25y^4\cdot(3y)}}\\&=\sqrt{\frac{-(4x^2)^2\cdot(2)}{(5y^2)^2\cdot(3y)}}\\&=\frac{4x^2i\sqrt{2}}{5y^2\sqrt{3y}}\cdot\frac{\sqrt{3y}}{\sqrt{3y}}\\&=\frac{4x^2i\sqrt{6y}}{15y^3}\end{aligned}$$

52. B: We can find the area of the shaded part by viewing the target as five separate circles of various sizes, one inside the other. We add the areas of the three shaded circles and subtract the areas of the two white circles. The area of a circle is πr^2, so the area of the largest circle (the entire target) is $\pi(5a)^2$. We subtract the white circle inside it, add the shaded circle inside that one, and so on:

$$\begin{aligned} A &= \pi(5a)^2 - \pi(4a)^2 + \pi(3a)^2 - \pi(2a)^2 + \pi(a)^2 \\ &= 25\pi a^2 - 16\pi a^2 + 9\pi a^2 - 4\pi a^2 + \pi a^2 \\ &= (25 - 16 + 9 - 4 + 1)\pi a^2 \\ &= 15\pi a^2 \end{aligned}$$

53. D: There are 90 two-digit numbers (all integers from, and including, 10 to 99). Of those, there are 13 multiples of 7: 14, 21, 28, 35, 42, 49, 56, 63, 70, 77, 84, 91, 98. Therefore, the probability of choosing a number that is a multiple of 7 is $\frac{13}{90}$.

54. C: First, use the properties of logarithms to solve for y:

$2\log_8 y + \log_8 4 = 2$	
$\log_8 y^2 + \log_8 4 = 2$	Use the power rule of logarithms to rewrite the first logarithm.
$\log_8 4y^2 = 2$	Use the product rule of logarithms to combine the two logarithms.
$4y^2 = 8^2$	Rewrite the equation using the logarithm rule that $\log_a b = c$ is equivalent to $a^c = b$.
$4y^2 = 64$	Simplify the square on the right side.
$y^2 = 16$	Divide both sides by 4.
$y = 4$	Take the positive square root of both sides.

Finally, substitute 4 for y in the expression $\log_y 64$ and simplify: $\log_4 64 = 3$ since $4^3 = 64$.

55. C: In Class 1, 27 students submitted late work, so the median is between the 13th and 14th piece of homework. Both the 13th and 14th fall on Day 4, so the median for Class 1 is 4. In Class 2, 23 students submitted late work, so the median is at the 12th piece of homework. This falls on Day 7. So, because $7 - 4 = 3$, the median number of days late in Class 1 is 3 less than the median number of days late in Class 2.

To find the mean late time for each class, find the sum of the late times and divide by the number of students turning in late work in each class. If the frequency of a one-day late time is 4, the number 1 is added four times (1×4), if frequency of a two-day late time is 5, the number 2 is added five times (2×5), and so on. So, to find the average turn-in time, divide the sum of the products of each late time and its corresponding frequency by the number of late turn-ins in each class. For Class 1, the mean late time is 5.22 days, which rounds to approximately 5 days.

$$\text{Mean} = \frac{4(1) + 5(2) + 3(3) + 2(4) + 3(5) + 1(6) + 1(7) + 2(9) + 4(10) + 2(12)}{4 + 5 + 3 + 2 + 3 + 1 + 1 + 2 + 4 + 2} = \frac{141}{27} \approx 5.22$$

For Class 2, the mean late time is 6.57, which rounds to approximately 7 days.

$$\text{Mean} = \frac{1(1) + 2(2) + 2(3) + 1(4) + 4(6) + 5(7) + 3(8) + 1(9) + 2(10) + 2(12)}{1 + 2 + 2 + 1 + 4 + 5 + 3 + 1 + 2 + 2} = \frac{151}{23} \approx 6.57$$

So, because $7 - 5 = 2$, the students in Class 2 turned in work 2 days later than in Class 1.

The mode late time is the date for which the frequency is the highest. For Class 1, the mode late time is 2 days, and for Class 2, the mode late time is 7 days.

The median late time for Class 1 is 4 and the mean is 4.96, so the median late time is less than the mean.

56. C: When the shirt is marked down by 25%, the cost of the shirt is 75% of its original price. Therefore, the reduced price of the shirt can be written as $\frac{75}{100}x$, or $\frac{3}{4}x$, where x is the original price. When discounted an extra 30%, the shirt costs 70% of the reduced price, or $\frac{70}{100}\left(\frac{3}{4}x\right)$, or $\frac{7}{10}\left(\frac{3}{4}x\right)$, which simplifies to $\frac{21}{40}x$. So, the final price is $\frac{21}{40}$ of the original price.

57. B: The first function shifts the graph of $y = \frac{1}{x}$ to the left one unit and down three units. The domain and range of $y = \frac{1}{x}$ are $\{x: x \neq 0\}$ and $\{y: y \neq 0\}$, so the domain and range of $y = \frac{1}{x+1} - 3$ are $\{x: x \neq -1\}$ and $\{y: y \neq -3\}$. The element –3 is not in its range.

The second function shifts the graph of $y = \sqrt{x}$ to the right two units and down three units. The domain and range of $y = \sqrt{x}$ are $\{x: x \geq 0\}$ and $\{y: y \geq 0\}$, so the domain and range of $y = \sqrt{x-2} - 3$ are $\{x: x \geq 2\}$ and $\{y: y \geq -3\}$. The domain contains the element 2, and the range contains the element –3.

The third function shifts the graph of $y = |x|$ to the left two units and down three units. The domain of $y = |x|$ is the set of all real numbers and the range is $\{y: y \geq 0\}$, so the domain of $y = |x - 1| + 3$ is the set of all real numbers and the range is $\{y: y \geq 3\}$. The element –3 is not in its range.

The domain of the piecewise fourth function is the set of all real numbers, and the range is $\{y: y \geq 2\}$. The range does not contain the element –3.

58. B: The line with fewer oscillations represents the sine function $f(x)$, and the line with more oscillations represents a cosine function $g(x)$. The amplitude of $f(x)$ is 1.5, and the amplitude of $g(x)$ is 3. The function $y = \sin x$ has a period of 2π, while the graph of function $f(x) = a_1 \sin(b_1 x)$ has a period of $\frac{8\pi}{2} = 4\pi$; therefore, $b_1 = \frac{2\pi}{4\pi} = 0.5$, which is not between –1 and 0. The graph of $g(x) = a_2 \cos(b_2 x)$ has a period of $\frac{8\pi}{8} = \pi$, so $b_2 = \frac{2\pi}{\pi} = 2$.

59. A: Calculate the final sales price of the rug at each store. Please note that the explanation below uses 1.08 instead of 0.08 for tax in order to avoid having to perform addition later. If 0.08 were to be used, only the amount of tax charged would result instead of the total cost of the product with tax included. Thus, 1.08 is used to make sure 108% of the product price is calculated.

$$1.08(0.7 \times \$296) = \$223.78 \text{ at Store A}$$
$$1.08(\$220 - \$10) = \$226.80 \text{ at Store B}$$
$$\$198 + \$35 = \$233 \text{ at Store C}$$

60. C: If 1 inch represents 25 feet, then 12 inches represents 300 feet because $12 \times 25 = 300$. Since there are 3 feet in a yard, 300 feet is the same as 100 yards. Therefore, the two points are 100 yards apart.

61. B: A score of 91 is one standard deviation above the mean ($84 + 7 = 91$). Since approximately 68% of the data is within one standard deviation of the mean, about 32% (100% − 68%) of the data is outside of one standard deviation within the mean. Normally distributed data is symmetric about the mean, which means that about 16% of the data lies below one standard deviation below the mean and about 16% of data lies above one standard deviation above the mean. Therefore, approximately 16% of the students scored 91 or higher. Since 16% of 250 is 40, about 40 students scored at least 91.

62. C: The inequality will be less than or equal to 25 because she only has $25 available to spend on her purchase.

63. C: Partitioned into rectangles with length of 1, the left and right Riemann sums will establish upper and lower bounds for the true area. The left Riemann sum:

$$1(6 + 7.5 + 8.5 + 9 + 8.75 + 7.75 + 6.5 + 5 + 3.75 + 3) = 65.75$$

The right Riemann sum:

$$1(7.5 + 8.5 + 9 + 8.75 + 7.75 + 6.5 + 5 + 3.75 + 3 + 3) = 62.75$$

Thus, the bounds on A are $62.75 < A < 65.75$.

64. B: The area of a triangle is $A = \frac{1}{2}bh$, where b and h are the lengths of the triangle's base and height, respectively. The base of the given triangle is x, but the height is not given. Since the triangle is a right triangle and the hypotenuse is given, the triangle's height can be found using the Pythagorean theorem.

$$x^2 + h^2 = 6^2$$
$$h = \sqrt{36 - x^2}$$

To find the area of the triangle in terms of x, substitute $\sqrt{36 - x^2}$ for the height and x for the base of the triangle into the area formula $\left(A = \frac{1}{2}bh\right)$:

$$A(x) = \frac{1}{2}(x)(\sqrt{36 - x^2})$$
$$A(x) = \frac{x\sqrt{36 - x^2}}{2}$$

65. C: The height of the ball is a function of time, so the equation can be expressed as $h(t) = -18t^2 + 72t + 4$, and the average rate of change can be found by calculating $\frac{h(3)-h(0)}{3-0}$.

$$\frac{[-18(3)^2 + 72(3) + 4] - [-18(0)^2 + 64(0) + 4]}{3}$$
$$= \frac{(-162 + 216 + 4) - (0 + 0 + 4)}{3}$$
$$= \frac{54}{3}$$
$$= 18$$

The average rate of change in the ball's height is 18 feet/second.

66. B: To find the integral, use u-substitution.

$$\int 4x^3 e^{x^4}\, dx$$

Let $u = x^4$ and then find du.

$$du = 4x^3 dx$$

Therefore, the u-substitution function becomes $\int e^u\, du$. Find the integral.

$$\int e^u\, du = e^u + C$$

Now, substitute x^4 back in for u to get the final answer.

$$e^{x^4} + C$$

67. C: The equation that can model this situation would have to have the amount of money Lex spends each week as the constant, or y-intercept, and the rate, or the slope, would be the amount of money he charges for each lawn he mows. Therefore, the best equation to model this situation is $y = 25x - 80$.

68. B: All regular polygons have rotational symmetry. The angle of rotation is the smallest angle by which the polygon can be rotated such that it maps onto itself; any multiple of this angle will also map the polygon onto itself. The angle of rotation for a regular polygon is the angle formed between two lines drawn from consecutive vertices to the center of the polygon. Since the vertices of a regular polygon lie on a circle, for a regular polygon with n sides, the angle of rotation measures $\frac{360°}{n}$. Therefore, a square has rotational symmetry about the angle 90° and its multiples. A regular hexagon has rotational symmetry about the angle 60° and its multiples. A regular octagon has rotational symmetry about 45° and its multiples. And a regular decagon has rotational symmetry about 36° and its multiples. Since 120° is a multiple of 60°, the correct answer is a regular hexagon.

69. C: In the box-and-whisker plot in choice A, the lowest value is 3, which is much too low, so choice A is not representative of the data from the stem and leaf plot.

To draw a pie chart, find the percentage of data contained in each of the ranges shown. There are 5 out of 20 numbers between 10 and 19, inclusive, so the percentage shown in the pie chart for that range of data is $\frac{5}{20} \times 100\% = 25\%$; there are 3 values between 20 and 29, inclusive, so the percentage of data for that sector is $\frac{3}{20} \times 100\% = 15\%$. Since the pie chart shows 30% for the 20–29 range, choice B is not representative of the data.

To draw a cumulative frequency histogram, find the cumulative frequency of the data.

Range	Frequency	Cumulative Frequency
10–19	5	5
20–29	3	8
30–39	6	14
40–49	6	20

The histogram shows the correct cumulative frequencies.

The data points in the line graph in choice D do not correspond to the data points given for the question.

70. A: By definition, when $f(x)$ and $g(x)$ are inverse functions, $f(g(x)) = g(f(x)) = x$. So, $f\big(g(b)\big) = b = -6$.

71. A: Use the FOIL method to multiply the binomials, and then combine like terms.

$$\begin{aligned}(2x - 20)(5x + 10) &= 10x^2 + 20x - 100x - 200 \\ &= 10x^2 - 80x - 200\end{aligned}$$

72. B: To solve the equation, write $x^4 + 64 = 20x^2$ in the quadratic form, then factor.

$$(x^2)^2 - 20(x^2) + 64 = 0$$

This trinomial can be factored as $(x^2 - 4)(x^2 - 16) = 0$. Each set of parentheses contains a difference of squares, which can be factored further: $(x + 2)(x - 2)(x + 4)(x - 4) = 0$. Use the zero product property to find the solutions to the equation.

$$\begin{array}{cccc} x + 2 = 0 & x - 2 = 0 & x + 4 = 0 & x - 4 = 0 \\ x = -2 & x = 2 & x = -4 & x = 4 \end{array}$$

Therefore, the solution to the equation is $x = \{-4, -2, 2, 4\}$.

73. D: The probability of an event is the number of possible occurrences of that event divided by the number of all possible outcomes. A student who is at least nine years old can be nine or ten years old, so the probability of randomly selecting a student at least nine years old is:

$$\frac{\text{number of nine- and ten-year old students}}{\text{total number of students}} = \frac{10 + 14}{10 + 9 + 13 + 10 + 14} = \frac{24}{56} = \frac{3}{7}$$

74. B: The graph of $f(x)$ is stretched vertically by a factor of 4 with respect to $y = \sin x$, so $a_1 = 4$. The graph of $g(x)$ is stretched vertically by a factor of 2 and is inverted with respect to the graph of $y = \cos x$, so $a_2 = -2$. Therefore, the statement $a_2 < 0 < a_1$ is true.

75. A: The vertex form of a quadratic equation is $y = a(x - h)^2 + k$, where $x = h$ is the parabola's axis of symmetry and (h, k) is the parabola's vertex. The vertex of the graph is $(-2, -1)$, so the equation can be written as $y = a(x + 2)^2 - 1$. The parabola passes through point (0,3), so $3 = a(0 + 2)^2 - 1$. Solve for a.

$$\begin{aligned} 3 &= a(0+2)^2 - 1 \\ 3 &= a(2)^2 - 1 \\ 3 &= 4a - 1 \\ 4 &= 4a \\ 1 &= a \end{aligned}$$

So, the vertex form of the parabola is $y = (x + 2)^2 - 1$. Write the equation in standard form, $y = ax^2 + bx + c$.

$$\begin{aligned} y &= (x+2)^2 - 1 \\ y &= (x+2)(x+2) - 1 \\ y &= (x^2 + 4x + 4) - 1 \\ y &= x^2 + 4x + 3 \end{aligned}$$

76. B: Multiply the second equation by 2 and combine it with the first equation to eliminate z.

$$\begin{array}{rrrrcr} & 3x & -\ y & +2z & = & 2 \\ + & -2x & +6y & -2z & = & 12 \\ \hline & x & +5y & & = & 14 \end{array}$$

Multiply the third equation by −1 and combine it with the original second equation to eliminate z.

$$\begin{array}{rrrrcr} & -x & +3y & -z & = & 6 \\ + & -2x & -2y & +z & = & 0 \\ \hline & -3x & +y & & = & 6 \end{array}$$

Multiply the equation from step one by 3 and combine to eliminate x.

$$\begin{array}{rrrcr} & 3x & +15y & = & 42 \\ + & -3x & +y & = & 6 \\ \hline & & 16y & = & 48 \\ & & y & = & 3 \end{array}$$

Substitute 3 for y in the equation from step one to find x.

$$\begin{aligned} x + 5(3) &= 14 \\ x + 15 &= 14 \\ x &= -1 \end{aligned}$$

Substitute –1 for x and 3 for y into the third original equation to find z.

$$\begin{aligned} 2(-1) + 2(3) - z &= 0 \\ -2 + 6 - z &= 0 \\ 4 - z &= 0 \\ z &= 4 \end{aligned}$$

Therefore, the solution to the system of equations is $(-1,3,4)$.

77. C: When a figure is reflected twice over non-parallel lines, the resulting transformation is a rotation about the point of intersection of the two lines of reflection. The two lines of reflection $y = -x + 1$ and $x = 0$ intersect at (0,1). So, $\Delta A''B''C''$ represents a rotation of ΔABC about the point (0,1). The angle of rotation is equal to twice the angle between the two lines of reflection when measured in a counterclockwise direction from the first to the second line of reflection. Since the angle between the lines or reflection measures 135°, the angle of rotation which is the composition of the two reflections measures 270°.

78. A: The inequality that represents this scenario is $n + 3p \leq 30$, where n is the number of notebooks and p is the number of boxes of pencils. To graph this inequality, find the intercepts of this linear inequality by making the inequality an equality and setting n and p equal to 0 and solving for the other variable.

$$\begin{aligned} (0) + 3p &= 30 \\ 3p &= 30 \\ p &= 10 \end{aligned}$$

$$\begin{aligned} n + 3(0) &= 30 \\ n &= 30 \end{aligned}$$

The intercepts are $n = 30$ and $p = 10$. The solid line through the two intercepts represents the maximum number of each item that may be purchased. Since this inequality represents the maximum he can purchase, all first-quadrant points below the line are also possible amounts within Ben's budget.

79. C: Will used the following calculations.

$$1 \text{ bag of flour } \times \frac{5 \text{ lb}}{1 \text{ bag}} \times \frac{16 \text{ oz}}{1 \text{ lb}} \times \frac{25 \text{ g protein}}{4 \text{ oz}} \times \frac{1 \text{ serving}}{50 \text{ g protein}} \approx \frac{5 \times 16 \times 25}{4 \times 50} = 10$$

So, Will should divide the flour into 10 equal portions to equal the weight of chicken that would contain 50 grams of protein.

80. C: If $f(x) = 10^x$ and $f(x) = 3$, then $3 = 10^x$. Since $\log_{10}x$ is the inverse of 10^x, $\log_{10}3 = \log_{10}(10^x) = x$. Therefore, $0.5 \approx x$.

81. B: There are three ways in which two women from the same department can be selected. Two women can be selected from the first department, two women can be selected from the second department, or two women can be selected from the third department.

Department 1	Department 2	Department 3
$\frac{12}{103} \times \frac{11}{102} = \frac{132}{10{,}506}$	$\frac{28}{103} \times \frac{27}{102} = \frac{756}{10{,}506}$	$\frac{16}{103} \times \frac{15}{102} = \frac{240}{10{,}506}$

Since any of these is a distinct possible outcome, the probability that two women will be selected from the same department is the sum of these outcomes.

$$\frac{132}{10{,}506}+\frac{756}{10{,}506}+\frac{240}{10{,}506}=\frac{1{,}128}{10{,}506}\approx 0.107$$

Converting this to a percentage, the probability that two women from the same department will be chosen is approximately 10.7%.

82. A: The revenue Jen receives from each method of sale is:

$$0.8\times 0.75\times \$10.50=\$6.30 \text{ from Store A}$$
$$0.8(\$11.00-\$1.50)=\$7.60 \text{ from Store B}$$
$$\$6.75+\$2.50-\$2.50=\$6.75 \text{ from Store C}$$

So, Store A will give the lowest revenue, Store C is next, and Store B brings the highest revenue during the sale.

83. D: Solve this equation by completing the square or by using the quadratic formula, $x=\frac{-b\pm\sqrt{b^2-4ac}}{2a}$. Here we will use the quadratic formula. First, set the equation equal to 0 by adding 2 to both sides. The equation $5x^2-4x+2=0$ has $a=5, b=-4, c=2$. Substitute these values into the quadratic formula and simplify.

$$x=\frac{-b\pm\sqrt{b^2-4ac}}{2a}$$
$$x=\frac{4\pm\sqrt{(-4)^2-4(5)(2)}}{2(5)}$$
$$x=\frac{4\pm\sqrt{16-40}}{10}$$
$$x=\frac{4\pm\sqrt{-24}}{10}$$
$$x=\frac{4\pm 2i\sqrt{6}}{10}$$
$$x=\frac{2\pm i\sqrt{6}}{5}$$

84. D: The center of the sphere is shared by the center of the cube, and each of the corners of the cube touches the surface of the sphere. Therefore, the diameter of the sphere is the line that passes through the center of the cube and connects one corner of the cube to the opposite corner on the opposite face. Notice in the illustration below that the diameter d of the sphere can be represented as the hypotenuse of a right triangle with a short leg measuring 1.5 units. (Since the volume of the cube is 3.375 cubic units, each of its sides measures $\sqrt[3]{3.375}=1.5$ or $\frac{3}{2}$ units.) Since leg c of the triangle is the diagonal of the base of the cube, its length can be found using the Pythagorean theorem: $\left(\frac{3}{2}\right)^2+\left(\frac{3}{2}\right)^2=c^2; c=\sqrt{\frac{18}{4}}=\frac{3\sqrt{2}}{2}$.

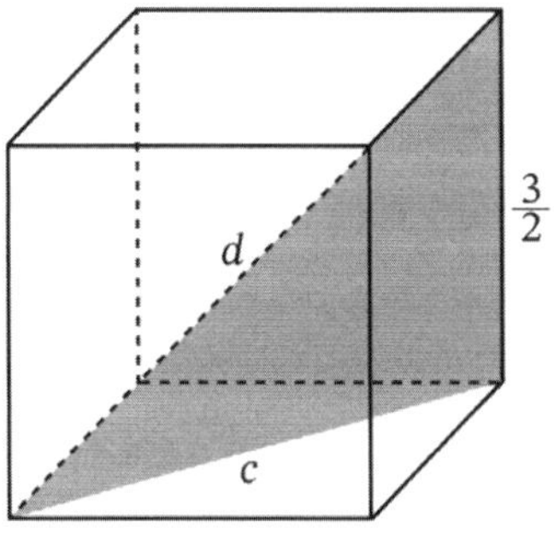

Use the Pythagorean theorem again to find d, the diameter of the sphere: $d^2 = \left(\frac{3\sqrt{2}}{2}\right)^2 + \left(\frac{3}{2}\right)^2$; $d = \sqrt{\frac{27}{4}} = \frac{3\sqrt{3}}{2}$. To find the volume of the sphere, use the formula $V = \frac{4}{3}\pi r^3$. Since the radius r of the sphere is half the diameter, $r = \frac{3\sqrt{3}}{4}$, and $V = \frac{4}{3}\pi\left(\frac{3\sqrt{3}}{4}\right)^3 = \frac{4}{3}\pi\left(\frac{81\sqrt{3}}{64}\right) = \frac{27\pi\sqrt{3}}{16}$ cubic units.

85. B: The ratio of revenue of new car sales to used car sales is 3 : 5. This means that the total revenue of cars sold (both new and used) is $3 + 5 = 8$. The used car sales are $\frac{5}{8}$ of the total sales:

$$\frac{5}{8} \times \$287{,}400 = \$179{,}625$$

86. B: This situation may be modeled by a geometric sequence, with a common ratio of 3 and initial value of 2. Substituting the common ratio and initial value into the formula $a_n = a_1 \times r^{n-1}$ gives $a_n = 2 \times 3^{n-1}$.

87. C: Find the points of intersection of the two graphs:

$$\begin{gathered} x^2 - 2x - 7 = x - 3 \\ x^2 - 3x - 4 = 0 \\ (x+1)(x-4) = 0 \\ x = -1 \qquad x = 4 \end{gathered}$$

So, the area is between the graphs on the interval $[-1,4]$. To determine which of the graphs is the upper or lower bound, pick a test point in the interval. Using $x = 0$ as the test point.

$$\begin{array}{cc} y = x^2 - 2x - 7 & y = x - 3 \\ y = 0^2 - 2(0) - 7 & y = 0 - 3 \\ y = -7 & y = -3 \end{array}$$

The finite region is bound at the top by the line $y = x - 3$ and at the bottom by $y = x^2 - 2x - 7$. The height of the region at point x is defined by $[(x - 3) - (x^2 - 2x - 7)]$, so the area is:

$$
\begin{aligned}
A &= \int_{-1}^{4} [(x-3) - (x^2 - 2x - 7)]dx \\
&= \int_{-1}^{4} (-x^2 + 3x + 4\,)\,dx \\
&= \left[-\frac{1}{3}x^3 + \frac{3}{2}x^2 + 4x\right]_{-1}^{4} \\
&= \left[-\frac{1}{3}(4)^3 + \frac{3}{2}(4)^2 + 4(4)\right] - \left[-\frac{1}{3}(-1)^3 + \frac{3}{2}(-1)^2 + 4(-1)\right] \\
&= \left[-\frac{64}{3} + 24 + 16\right] - \left[\frac{1}{3} + \frac{3}{2} - 4\right] \\
&= \frac{56}{3} - \left(-\frac{13}{6}\right) \\
&= \frac{125}{6}
\end{aligned}
$$

88. B: The movement of the weight can be described by graphing height h in inches as a function of time t in seconds. Notice that the height is 0.5 in above the table at time 0 since the weight was pulled down 3 inches from its starting position 3.5 inches above the table. The spring fluctuates 3 inches above and below its equilibrium point, so its maximum height is 6.5 inches above the table. The graph represents a cosine curve that has been inverted, stretched vertically by a factor of 3, and shifted up 3.5 units; also, the graph has been compressed horizontally, with a period of 1.5 rather than 2π. So, the height of the weight on the spring as a function of time is $h = -3\cos\left(\frac{4}{3}\pi t\right) + 3.5$.

89. B: The volume of Natasha's tent can be found by using the volume formula for a square pyramid, $V = \frac{1}{3}Bh = \frac{1}{3}s^2h$, where B is the area of the base, s is the side length of the square base, and h is the height of the pyramid. Therefore, the volume of her tent is $\frac{x^2h}{3}$. If she were to increase the length of each side of the square base by 1 ft, the tent's volume would be $\frac{(x+1)^2h}{3} = \frac{(x^2+2x+1)(h)}{3} = \frac{x^2h+2xh+h}{3} = \frac{x^2h}{3} + \frac{2xh+h}{3}$. Notice this is the volume of Natasha's tent, $\frac{x^2h}{3}$, increased by $\frac{2xh+h}{3}$.

90. D: Working the problem backwards, start by adding \$12 to \$17 to find out how much money she had before the movie.

$$\$12 + \$17 = \$29$$

Therefore, Jody had \$29 before she went to the movies. This was half of the money she made at the bake sale.

$$2 \times \$29 = \$58$$

So, Jodi made \$58 at the bake sale.